TRAMPOLINING

N.N.

TRAMPOLINING
The Skills of the Game

BRIAN AND ERIKA PHELPS

THE CROWOOD PRESS

First published in 1990 by
The Crowood Press
Ramsbury, Marlborough,
Wiltshire SN8 2HE

British Library Cataloguing in Publication Data

Phelps, Erika
   Trampolining: the skills of the game.
   1. Trampolining
   I. Title II. Phelps, Brian
   796.4'7

   ISBN 1 85223 363 X

Acknowledgements

The authors wish to thank Geoffrey C. Phillips (LBIPP, LMPA) for
the photography, Robert Thorne, Claire Ede, Mark Beverley and
Thomas Harris for acting as demonstrators and Joy Cottingham,
Jane Williams and Marjorie Curtis for their help in preparing the
script.

Line-drawings (except Fig 2) by Margaret Cree

Front cover photograph by Allsport

Set in 10 on 12pt Helvetica Light

Typeset by Action Typesetting Ltd, Gloucester
Printed and bound in Great Britain by
BPCC Hazell Books Ltd, Aylesbury

Contents

My career in trampolining spanned over thirteen years and the undisputed highlight of that exciting time was becoming British Mens' Trampoline Champion in 1985. Sharing my great moment was my coach Brian Phelps — Olympic high diving bronze medallist, who became European Diving Champion at the age of fourteen and British Mens' Trampoline Champion at the age of fifteen. Brian knows the requirements of success in sport: dedication; hard work; single-mindedness and self-belief. He can bring out the talent in any individual and he can also motivate the best performance an individual can possibly achieve. Excellence is his aim.

The beauty of this inspiring contribution to the wonderful sport of trampolining is it's co-authorship with his daughter Erika. Together they created an era in British Trampolining, motivating coaches and performers throughout the world. Much of the text relates to their vast experience together developing methods of learning in safety, and of course Brian has coached literally hundreds of children of all abilities and through his experience has learned to recognise the common denominators of faults, fears and phobias.

This book will be a must in every coach's library. It describes correct progressive learning from the beginning, suggests development to suit individual needs and gives invaluable advice in the subtle techniques required in coaching excellence. I am sure that it will encourage participation and benefit individuals of all ages and all standards in trampolining.

Nigel Rendell
British Trampoline Champion 1985—6

A remarkably versatile and talented athlete, Brian Phelps won six gold medals for diving in Olympic, European and Commonwealth games, as well as being former British Trampolining Champion at both senior and junior levels. Having represented Great Britain on fifty-four occasions, he is now a highly respected full-time trampolining coach.

His many successful students have included his daughter, Erika Phelps, who has had a distinguished trampolining career. Among her many honours, she was British Champion in both the under-13 and under-15 age groups and represented Great Britain in both the World and European Championships. In 1980 she won a bronze medal at the World Championships and was also the winner of the World Cup.

Introduction

Trampolining started as a competitive sport in the United States in the 1950s. George Nissen marketed the first trampolines, and was very much involved in the early development of the sport. Most of the early champions were Americans, but now the sport is dominated by Europeans. Trampolining came to Great Britain in 1959 when Ted Blake brought the first Nissen Trampoline into the country and installed it at Loxford School in Essex.

These early trampolines consisted of a plain nylon bed with rubber cables connecting it to the frame. It was soon discovered that the performance of the trampoline could be enhanced by putting holes in the bed. These holes allowed a significantly greater downward force to be exerted on the trampoline. This is because the air beneath could now move freely up through the bed rather than damping the movement caused by the performer landing on the trampoline. The first webbed beds were made from two-inch webbing with a half-inch hole (*see* Fig 2). At this time (the early 1960s) the largest frame size was about fourteen by nine feet (4.5 × 2.7m). During competitions four spotters were required, one at each end and one at each side. In the early days there were no crash mats at either end.

The sport developed very quickly and as the manoeuvres increased in difficulty, so more height was required from the performer. To make this possible the webbing was reduced in thickness and the holes were enlarged — the webbing was reduced to one inch and very soon to half an inch.

The dramatic improvement in apparatus and thus expertise and quality of performance saw the beginning of a new era in trampolining. The new half-inch bed gave so much more power that the frame size had to be increased and the 'Goliath' was born — its size being approximately sixteen by ten feet (4.8 × 3m) and four feet (1.2m) off the ground. However, the larger frame size and more powerful beds inevitably meant more danger; accordingly the safety aspects of the sport had to be reviewed. This led to the introduction of spotting decks at the end of trampolines. These decks are padded with large crash mats making the sport much safer — and as more difficult manoeuvres could now be performed, tariffs became progressively higher until the 'magic 10.0' tariff was achieved. (The tariff is the degree of difficulty and the term is explained in Chapter 6).

During the same period of rapid development in the sport, the British Trampoline Federation (BTF) was formed in 1963. It took over from the Amateur Gymnastics Association (AGA) and has governed the sport since that time.

Everyone involved in trampolining at this time thought that the ultimate in equipment had been reached. Any more development in achievement was expected through the talent of the performer and good coaching. This was proved wrong, as 1978 saw the introduction of the 8mm (0.3in) webbed bed, closely followed by the 6mm (0.2in) bed. Trampolinists once again had further opportunities which could be exploited.

Fig 1   Helen Channon performing a straight back.

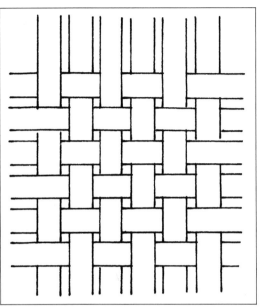

Fig 2   Trampoline bed webbing.

Even young children were able to gain the height to perform complicated skills and consequently international performers became much younger. Amidst the delight of the achievements of these younger performers, however, coaches seemed unaware of the potential stress on the immature human frame — measures to prevent this stress are now an integral part of trampoline coaching.

During the past twenty years Great Britain has stamped its mark on international trampolining with performers such as:

Paul Luxon	Britain's first ever World Champion (1972)
Erika Phelps	1980 World Cup Champion and third in the 1980 World Championships at the age of 13
Stewart Matthews	1980 World Champion
Carl Furrer	1982 World Champion
Sue Shotton	1984 World Champion
Andrea Holmes	Second in World Championships 1986, 1988
Stewart Matthews Carl Furrer }	1980 World Synchro Champions
Andrea Holmes Penny Thomas }	Gold medallist, 1983 World Synchro Championships
Sue Shotton Kirsty McDonald }	1984 World Synchro Champions
Andrea Holmes Sachelle Halford }	Silver medallist, 1988 World Synchro Championships

1 Body Conditioning

As the title of the chapter suggests, the body has to be conditioned for the activities and skills it is expected to perform. Conditioning, or body preparation, is much neglected in trampolining. Although trampolining assists the body by providing time in which to perform skills, conditioning is important as it trains the body to carry out the manoeuvres as quickly as possible. To acquire this speed of muscular action the brain must be aware and the body strong and supple. To be able to train for long periods, the trampolinist must be in good aerobic condition; this requires good cardio-vascular fitness. Sustaining training over several years requires body prep-aration (which is also one method of injury prevention).

Body preparation can be divided into six sections, each of which should be regarded as an essential part of the trampolinist's training programme and which should take priority over actual bouncing, both in terms of time and effort. These six components are:

1. Cardio-vascular fitness.
2. Suppleness.
3. Strength within the range of movement.
4. Speed of muscular action and co-ordination.
5. Psychological attitude to training.
6. Diet.

The order of importance of these components varies between individuals as some people may be naturally stronger or more supple than others. Basically we each have a different genetic make-up which results in varying psychological and physio-logical weaknesses and strengths. Since a whole book could be written on this topic alone, the six components of body preparation are discussed briefly in relation to the life-style of a trampolinist.

Fig 3   Clare Haydon (née Fricker) performing a double back somersault.

CARDIO-VASCULAR FITNESS

This enables the trampolinist to train for long periods of time with maximum physical effort. To improve cardio-vascular fitness, jogging, skipping or cycling should be performed at a moderate pace for at least thirty minutes each day (assuming the trampolinist trains five days out of seven). Trampolining is an aerobic form of exercise and so uses energy within the muscles; however, the lungs and heart are not exercised adequately by trampolining alone and so stamina is not developed unless cardio-vascular exercises are carried out. Cycling or jogging both burn off excess fat and so are necessary if weight loss is required. Training does not exclusively consist of bouncing; only three such sessions are needed in a week:

Monday	Body preparation
Tuesday	Body preparation
Wednesday	Bouncing
Thursday	Body preparation
Friday	Bouncing

Those fortunate enough to be able to fit in two sessions daily could carry out body preparation on all five days.

SUPPLENESS

From as early on as possible when ligaments are most pliable, the body should be stretched to provide a good range of movement. For a trampolinist suppleness does not have to be as excessive as for a gymnast. However, the ankles, Achilles tendons, hamstrings, quadriceps, hips and shoulders should all have excellent range. Stretching should follow the warm-up and not be carried out as part of it; it should be performed slowly and gradually — jerking actions will only shorten the muscles. It should take place daily, always before bouncing.

STRENGTH WITHIN THE RANGE OF MOVEMENT

The parts of the body that are stretched must be strengthened twice weekly on a regular basis. Ankles in particular should be supple and strong. Stretching, flexing and rotating them (both inwards and outwards) should be carried out daily with twenty or thirty repetitions for each exercise. Toe raises — raising and lowering the body-weight on the ball of the foot — should also be performed, preferably on a bench. This will achieve good stretching of the Achilles tendons. Often one ankle is weaker than the other, so the exercise should be done on both feet at the same time and also on alternate feet. Quadriceps, biceps and shoulders should also be strengthened as well as stretched. Upper and lower abdominal muscles and upper and lower back muscles should be exercised separately when strengthened.

SPEED OF MUSCULAR ACTION AND CO-ORDINATION

A circuit containing strengthening and speed exercises performed against a stop-watch should be used to improve muscular action and co-ordination speeds. The circuit should be designed and the performer timed to assess how long it takes to complete. The performer should then try to reduce this time, simultaneously increasing the amount of times the circuit is repeated. Further progression can be attained by increasing the length or degree of difficulty of the circuit. All the muscle groups should be exercised and the exercises should be completed correctly — if they are not, improvement will not occur. The circuit will also enhance stamina and fitness. The emphasis should be on performing the exercises well and at speed.

PSYCHOLOGICAL ATTITUDE TO TRAINING

A positive attitude should be encouraged by the coach through punctuality, regular training and a good work-rate. Targets should be realistic and so should be ful-filled; body preparation should eventually become self-disciplined. There is no sub-stitute for hard work, for which a fit, refined body is needed. Self-discipline will come with guidance and the desire to succeed. However, a young trampolinist will need direction.

DIET

Diet is not the reduction of body-weight but rather the pattern of eating which provides energy for exercise and sustains a healthy body with the minimum of weight gain. Excess fat is unnecessary, unhealthy and a distinct disadvantage to the trampolinist, both in terms of activity and appearance. Males and females, either pre-pubescent or post-pubescent, all vary in their food-intake requirements. In general we all eat and drink more than we need; indeed feeding is habitual. Greedy children often become fat adults. Moderate eating is therefore the ideal, provided the following points are borne in mind.

Breakfast is the most important meal of the day. Carbohydrates and proteins are of major importance in a diet, but fat should only be included in very small portions. Most foods already contain the fat we require, so butter, cheese, cream and fried foods are best removed from the diet. Red meat contains more fat than protein and so should also be avoided. Water is the best liquid to drink. Vitamin C tablets are a valuable supplement to all athletes and your doctor can advise you which supple-ments you will require if you detest certain foods. To sum up, here are some hints for good eating: wholemeal bread; low-fat spreads; baked potatoes; salad; fish; white meat; fresh fruit and vegetables; plenty of water.

2   Safety and Basic Mechanics

Trampolining is a fascinating and exciting sport both to watch and learn. It has been designed so that the performer can explore the potential of body movement through the air. The trampoline provides the opportunity to perform safely movements or skills which would otherwise be impossible.

There is no reason why the sport should be classed as dangerous provided the following safety rules are applied at all times.

Fig 4   Erika Phelps showing superb flexibility in the pike shape.

SAFETY

1.   When the trampoline is set up, all the chains below it should be checked to ensure that they are tight. Crash mats should be put at each end of the trampoline on stable pieces of apparatus. The springs should be checked to ensure that they are all in position and facing the correct way, with their hooks pointing downwards. The trampoline should be set up away from other activities such as ball and racket games. A football or shuttlecock flying on to the trampoline in the middle of a routine is both off-putting and dangerous. It is also inadvisable for the trampoline to be set up near a wall. Spotters do a much better job than a wall − if they are concentrating!
2.   One of the most important rules is that however competent trampolinists are, or think they are, they should never practise without the supervision of a British Trampolining Federation (BTF) coach. If this rule is remembered then the performer will always be covered by insurance should an accident ever occur.
3.   The correct clothing should be worn. For men this consists of shorts and a T-shirt or a leotard and shorts while women should wear either a leotard or shorts and a T-shirt. Tracksuits are suitable so long as those with zips are avoided − the zips can dig into the trampolinist when performing manoeuvres. Footwear is very important as modern trampoline webbing is fine with large holes. Performers should never

trampoline barefoot as toes can get caught in the holes very easily. Training shoes or plimsolls should not be worn and most performers are happy wearing gymnastic shoes or even just socks. As performers start to gain more height they may need to wear more than one pair of socks as the webbing can make the heels quite tender after a long training session.

4. As previously mentioned, performers should never bounce on a trampoline whilst alone. Apart from the coach there must be at least four other people standing at the sides and ends of the trampoline to assist the performer should he or she come too near the edge of the trampoline. These people are called 'spotters' and should be familiar with trampolining and the level of performance in operation.

5. Jewellery should never be worn on the trampoline. These items can be lethal objects to the performer and the spotters or coach.

6. Performers should mount and dismount the trampoline with great care, avoiding the springs and being aware of slippery or loose frame pads. Performers should not jump from the trampoline to the floor. When bouncing on a trampoline, the muscles, ligaments and tendons in the body are all conditioned to soft landings. To suddenly jump onto a very hard surface from the height of a trampoline could thus cause serious injury.

7. Trampolinists should always bounce near the middle of the bed. If straying or 'pinging' over to the side near the springs occurs, then the bounce must be 'killed' at once. (This is described in detail later on in the chapter).

8. Performers should never attempt new skills unless their coach feels that they are ready for it. When teaching a new skill, the coach may physically support the performer or may choose other safety methods, such as a crash mat or safety harness. Trampolinists should never attempt a new manoeuvre without applying these safety methods and should always ensure that they have perfected the required work-ups for the skill they are learning.

9. Performers should not 'double bounce' on a trampoline with another person unless they are experts. This is dangerous, particularly for the older and heavier performer and should be left to the most advanced performers.

The Crash Mat

The crash mat is very thick, covered in canvas with a sponge interior. Crash mats come in various thicknesses, sometimes being as thick as 0.5 – 0.6m (1.5 – 2ft), with a surface area of approximately 1 – 1.5m^2 (11 – 16ft^2). Although quite large, they are reasonably light making them easy to handle. Their usefulness should never be underestimated.

Crash mats are soft to land on, so performers learning new moves will be much more confident knowing that if they have a bad landing it will not be uncomfortable – confidence on take-off is an important safety factor when learning new moves. The crash mat also kills the springiness of the trampoline which is again very useful when learning new moves. When performers attempt a manoeuvre for the first time the last thing on their minds is what they will do after landing (especially if it is a back drop landing). A bad landing means that the recoil of the trampoline could cause a performer to 'ping' off onto the floor. Crash mats were not used as much years ago, but as trampolines are much more powerful today, a small mistake in the movement of the hips is multiplied, so trampolinists and coaches are a lot more safety conscious.

Not only are crash mats used when learning new moves, but they are also pushed in for new combinations. Performers must learn how to work into and work out of every new manoeuvre. So, for example, after a performer has mastered a double full without using a crash mat the next progression will be a back somersault tucked with the performer learning how to work into a double full. The performer executes the tuck back and the coach pushes the crash mat in for the double full, as it is when learning the work-up that a performer is most likely to make a mistake. The manoeuvre learned after the double full may be a barani, so in this case the performer would do a tuck back into a double full with the crash mat being pushed in for the barani. This is the safe way to build up combinations.

The person pushing in the crash mat (whether the coach or a fellow performer) must be aware of where the performer is going to land, and so must make sure they push the crash mat right under the performer. If a performer lands on the edge of a crash mat he or she may go over on his or her ankle — this defeats the object of a safety mat; however, it rarely happens so long as the person pushing in the mat is always alert.

If these safety aspects are all borne in mind each time training is carried out on the trampoline, the performer will hopefully have a safe and enjoyable career in trampolining.

BASIC MECHANICS

Like everything else on earth, man is subject to certain laws of mechanics, and it is vitally important for trampolinists to have a basic understanding of the principles which may either assist or limit the sort of movements that can be performed during trampolining.

These laws are numerous and extremely complex, and therefore only those that are most important to the performer are dealt with in detail here.

Gravity

The human body, like all other objects, is subject to the gravitational pull of the Earth. The trampoline merely provides a limited opportunity to overcome such attraction. Simply stated, gravity means that 'what goes up must come down!'

Centre of Gravity

All objects possess a centre of gravity. In a perfectly even-shaped object, like a ball, the centre of gravity will be located exactly in the middle. In an object as fluid as man however, the centre of gravity is an imaginary point about which the weight and distribution of all parts of the body are equally located. In general, for a person standing upright with both hands at his or her sides, the centre of gravity will be located slightly below the navel, and at a point directly above the feet. Should he or she bend at the waist, whilst maintaining his or her balance, his or her centre of gravity will be located outside the body, but still directly above the feet. This concept may be a difficult one to understand, but will become more apparent to the performer as he or she gains experience of the more difficult skills.

Action and Reaction

Isaac Newton's third law of motion states that 'for every action there is an equal and opposite reaction'. This means for the trampolinist that the amount of effort put into the trampoline, and the manner in which it is done, will be reflected in the amount of height gained and the manner and direction of travel. This law also affects the type of movements that are performed when in the air — if at the top of a straight bounce the arms were both swung vigorously forwards and downwards to the sides of the body, then the body would tilt backwards in an attempt to spin in the opposite direction to the arms.

Rotation and Gyration

Rotation refers to that action where the body turns around an imaginary pole or line that stretches from one side of the body to the other, for instance as in a forward or backward rolling action or somersault. Gyration refers to the action where the body turns or spins around an imaginary line running from the head through to the soles of the feet, for example as in pirouetting or twisting. When the performer starts to rotate (somersault) or gyrate (twist) it must be noted that it is impossible to change the direction of these motions once in the air. The performer, however, may choose to speed up the somersault by altering the shape of the body (the smaller the body, the faster it will rotate and the longer the body, the slower it will rotate). This applies equally to twisting — if the performer wishes to speed up a twist then the arms are brought in close to the waist or

chest whereas to slow down the twist the arms must be taken away from the body and straight out to the sides.

Once contact with the bed has been lost, there is nothing that can be done to increase the amount of height or travel produced on take-off. There is nothing that can be done to decrease it either. Thus, if a large mistake is made on take-off there is really very little that can be done other than to assume the shape the body will be in for the required landing.

BOUNCING AND BASIC JUMPS

Straight Bouncing

Once on the trampoline the first thing a performer must learn to do is to bounce and then stop, which is called 'killing the bed' or 'killing the bounce'. This is very important for safety reasons as if the performer loses control slightly, one more bounce may result in the performer nearing the edge of the trampoline or even coming off it completely. In this situation the performer must kill his bounce immediately — this is done by bending the knees suddenly and tensioning the leg muscles to maintain an angle at the knee (*see* Figs 5 & 6). This sudden knee bend absorbs the rebound of the trampoline bed.

It is not easy to master high bouncing with control. The secret is in the technique. Firstly the performer should never try and bounce too high too quickly and should try to stay near the centre of the trampoline. On take-off the arms must swing past the waist and lift up above the head. The arms may need to be held for a split second at the top of each bounce so that they pass the

Figs 5 & 6   Killing the bounce.

Fig 6

waist at the correct time for the next bounce. This slight pause depends on how high the performer is — the higher the performer is, the longer the arms will need to be kept still at the top of each bounce. If the performer is just starting off and bouncing very low then there may be no need for the arms to be kept still at the top of the bounce at all. The arms must swing loosely in order to maintain balance. The body must also be tensed around the middle at the bottom of each bounce — this body tension (or tightening of the muscles) helps to keep the performer near the middle of the trampoline. The torso should be kept straight with the eyes glancing down towards the edge of the bed, taking care not to drop the head downwards.

Once straight, controlled bouncing has been mastered, along with the ability to kill the bounce correctly, a very gradual build-up of height can be aimed for. The per-

former must be very aware of keeping the body in a straight line for as long as possible before hitting the trampoline. If the performer breaks the body-line too early by bending the knees and turning the feet, it is called 'stamping' the bed. It is most commonly done when a performer tries to gain more height. The torso is usually brought forwards when stamping the trampoline and because of this large amount of body movement, balance and height will probably be lost. Once the habit of stamping has been formed it takes very fine co-ordination to break it. Remember: it is not the amount of effort put into stamping the bed that determines the height, but the speed at which the knees are straightened and the legs reach full extension. It is therefore clear that the effort goes to the wrong places when the performer stamps the bed.

Three Basic Shaped Jumps

The next stage involves putting shapes into the basic bounce. It is at this stage, when learning the tuck, pike and straddle jumps, that trampolinists may find it harder to stay in balance − this is very normal however, so they should not become impatient. If performers find that they are falling either forward or backward at the end of the jump then they must be creating rotation. If they do not reach their arms above their heads (as in Fig 5) before the shape of the jump is formed then they will be off-balance at the end of the jump. (The reach to the top of the bounce is called 'phasing'.) If the arms are not raised above the head and kept still to phase before the jump, or if the head is down, then a minute amount of forward rotation will have been created − this will be enough to put the performer off-balance at the end of the jump. Alternatively if the arms are jerked up above the head and overreach past the line of the head, then the trampolinist will create a small amount of backward rotation. This backward rotation can also be created if the legs are brought up during the jump before the arms have been raised above the head and when the shoulders are pulled back slightly out of line.

In any jump the arms must be lifted smoothly above the head as this phasing neutralises any rotation. The arms are then lowered to the required position for the shape that is being performed as the legs are lifted, also taking up their required shape. The shape must be attained at the top of the bounce after the slight phasing. Trampolinists must be careful not to phase for too long otherwise they will be assuming the position when they should be preparing for the next bounce − this does not look tidy and will not leave sufficient time to resume a straight body position before landing.

Tuck Jump (Fig 7)

After the arms have reached over the head the body must first phase, showing full extension. The arms are then dropped as the knees and waist are bent and the thighs make contact with the chest. The hands must be clasped together around the middle of the shins with the elbows tucked in close to the legs. A vertical line should be apparent from the knees to the toes.

Straddle Jump (Fig 8)

The take-off is the same as for the tuck jump and the phasing is just as important. The body folds acutely at the hips and the legs are lifted wide apart with one hand touching each outstretched foot. The back must be as flat as possible to show good amplitude (*see* the Glossary) and not hunched. Good form should include a lifted head, straight arms and perfectly stretched legs.

Pike Jump (Fig 9)

This is usually the hardest jump to control because unlike the tucked position which is quick and easy to complete and the straddle where the legs help to balance any lateral instability, any slight wobble is hard to correct or disguise after take-off. Everything has to be very accurate. If the pike is not following another jump then the performer should pick a well-controlled, straight bounce in which to perform it.

First the arms are lifted above the head very smoothly. After the body has shown its full extension, the performer folds at the hips as in the straddle jump but with the

Fig 7   Tuck jump.

Fig 8 Straddle jump.

Fig 9 Pike jump.

legs held firmly together, the hands touching the toes and keeping a flat back. The position is held for a split second and then smoothly a straight body-line is resumed, with the arms swinging past the waist in preparation for the next bounce.

Twist Jumps

These jumps are also useful to the beginner. Twisting is dealt with in more detail later on (*see* Chapter 3 and Chapter 5), but as we are discussing the basic jumps, the half- and full-twist jumps must also be included.

In order to perform the half-twist jump, the performer must leave the trampoline as if a straight jump is being performed. Just as the feet are about to leave the trampoline bed, the arms, shoulders and head must be pulled back very smoothly in the direction of the desired twist. The arms must stay above the head throughout the half twist. The main difference between the half- and full-twist jumps is that for the half twist the shoulders hardly need to be pulled back at all, whereas for the full-twist jump the shoulders need to be pulled back a bit more. People used to believe that if they wrapped in (brought both arms or one arm into the chest), they would twist faster — this is true, however it puts the body off-balance and so the arms are best kept above the head whilst in flight during twisting jumps.

LANDING POSITIONS

After the three basic shaped jumps and the half- and full-twist jumps are mastered, the trampolinist progresses to learn the basic landing positions. These are initially performed on their own and then eventually the trampolinist learns to twist and somersault to and from them. Very competent trampolinists are even able to double somersault in and out of specific landing positions, so in the early learning stages both coach and performer must be very aware of correct technique so as not to hinder progress later on.

Generally there are five landing positions — on the knees, on the hands and knees, on the seat, on the front and on the back. The knee drop is generally omitted these days as it is of little value to the performer and takes great body strength to perform without incurring injury to the back. The hands and knees drop is however valuable. It is a progression towards the front drop and also the somersault and is safe unlike the knee drop. The other three landing positions are all used in competitive routines and are the landing positions for more advanced skills and their work-ups.

Knee Drop (Fig 10)

As mentioned earlier it is very inadvisable even to attempt the knee drop; however, the correct way to perform it is as follows. It is very nearly impossible to perform a knee drop safely from any height, so it is important to stay low. The take-off is the same as with other jumps where the arms are lifted up above the head. The knees are then bent to a right angle and the arms are dropped down by the sides. The body-line should be held in complete tension, and very slightly piked (this is called a 'dished' shape). To return to the feet, the arms are lifted up as in a normal bounce and the legs straightened without the chest dropping. A performer should *never* attempt to somersault into or out of the knee drop.

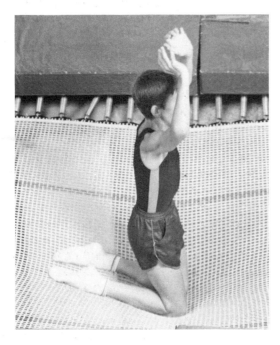

Fig 10   The correct landing for a knee drop.

Fig 11   Take-off for a seat drop.

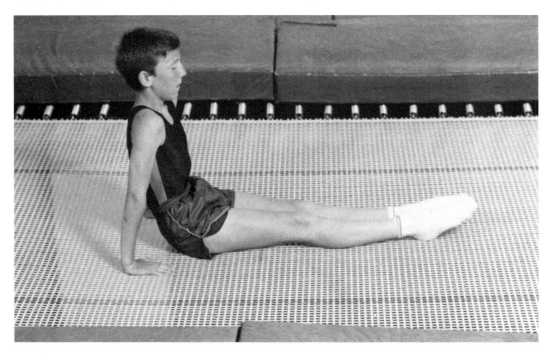

Fig 12   Seat drop landing position (with the fingers pointing forwards).

16

Seat Drop (Figs 11 & 12)

Although when landing in a seat drop, the body is in the same upright position as in a straight bounce, it does require a small amount of rotation to be performed successfully. Thus, as the performer leaves the bed on a seat drop take-off the arms should be lifted up and slightly past the line of the body to create a small amount of back rotation. This rotation is needed because as the legs are lifted for the seat drop landing position, the body automatically moves forward (due to action and reaction). Consequently, if no rotation was created the performer's chest would be too far forward on landing.

After the correct take-off has been performed the arms are brought down sideways and placed on each side of the body slightly behind the line of the hips, with the fingers pointing forwards, towards the toes. The hands, hips, and backs of the legs and heels must all come into contact with the trampoline at the same time. If the heels hit the bed first then either the legs were not lifted high enough, or insufficient rotation was created at the take-off stage. If, however, the hips land first followed by the legs and heels then too much rotation has been created. It is therefore important to have the fingers pointing towards the toes — if a performer were to create too much rotation and the fingers were pointing in the wrong direction, pressure would be on the elbow joint. With the fingers pointing in the correct direction, the elbows can simply bend if the legs touch the trampoline after the hips, and so no pressure is put on the elbows. By pushing from the hands and with a slight movement forwards of the shoulders a standing position will be reached.

Hands and Knees Drop (Fig 13)

Although this is never used in a competitive routine, the hands and knees drop is an excellent work-up for the front drop and the somersault. As it is a work-up it does not need a great deal of height to begin with — in fact when first learning the manoeuvre, it is a good idea for it to be attempted from a standing position. The performer stands in the middle of the trampoline simultaneously dropping the chest and head and bending the knees. There should be a right angle between the thighs and calves and between the shoulders and chest.

If insufficient rotation is produced or if the chest is not dropped far enough, the hands will land after the knees and the hip angle will be too acute (less than ninety degrees). This is called 'landing short'. It is also important not to have the elbows locked — if the performer produces too much rotation or 'overturns' the move, landing will be hands first, putting too much stress on the elbow joints if they are locked. If the arms are too bent however, the performer would land first on the hands and then the face! It is therefore important to strike a balance between the two.

To return to a standing position after performing the hands and knees drop, the trampolinist must push off the bed with the fingertips, lifting the chest at the same time and extending the legs.

Front Drop (Fig 14)

The take-off for the front drop is very similar to that of the hands and knees drop, therefore the latter is used as a progression. One of the best ways to learn the correct take-off is to do two consecutive hands and knees drops without returning to the feet and keeping the back parallel to the

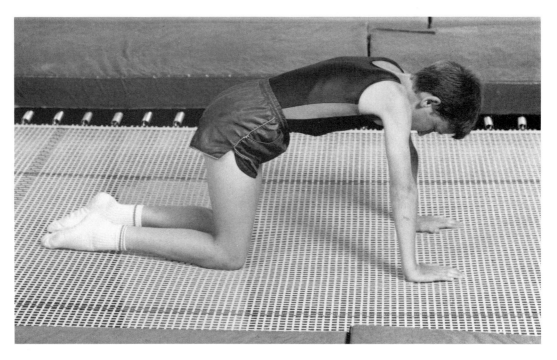

Fig 13   Hands and knees drop.

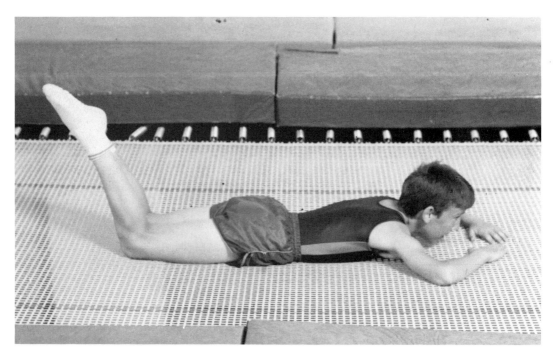

Fig 14   Front drop landing position.

trampoline. The next step is to do the same again, but before contact with the trampoline is made, the legs and arms are extended to their correct positions for the front drop. The legs in a front drop should be bent while the arms should be bent at the elbows with the elbows pointing out to the sides, level with the shoulders. The movement must be timed in such a way that the hands, arms, chest, abdomen and thighs all land on the trampoline at the same time.

After the performer gets a feel for the landing position of the front drop and masters standing (by pushing the arms straight and flicking the legs straight on leaving the bed), the front drop from standing can be attempted and the height gradually built up. The trampolinist often feels much safer performing the first few front

Fig 15   Take-off for a back drop.

Fig 16   Back drop landing position.

Safety and Basic Mechanics

drops from standing on a crash mat or a large piece of foam. This is also safer for the beginner.

Back Drop (Figs 15 & 16)

For this move, the arms swing past the waist and are brought upwards quickly to just below the ear-line. It is the action of stopping the arms after they have been swung up vigorously that creates the rotation for the back drop (this is an example of transfer of momentum). The further back the arms are before they are arrested, the more rotation is created. For a back drop the arms are stopped in mid-swing just below the line of the ears as the hips are pushed gently forwards and upwards. Often beginners will not get enough rotation for fear of overturning the movement and landing on their heads —

they either push their hips back instead of up and do not swing their arms up fast enough.

On landing, the body should be bent at the hips to a ninety degree angle, the arms should be parallel with the legs and the head should be on the trampoline. It is very important for the head to be on the trampoline in these early stages as it will be more difficult to progress to somersaulting out of a back drop if this position cannot be mastered. To stand, the legs must be pushed gently forwards and downwards as the body straightens out. As with the front drop, the back drop may be performed in a tucked, piked or straight position. It must be remembered however, that the body rotates much faster when tucked or piked and so less rotation must be created on take-off if a tucked or piked front or back drop is to be performed.

3   Twisting and Basic Routines

TWISTING

Having mastered the basic drops, the trampolinist may progress to add a twist (either half or full) before and/or after the landing position, during the performance of the move. The most important techniques are illustrated here, but any of the landing positions may be performed with either a half twist, full twist, or a one-and-a-half twist into or out of the move.

Fig 17   Phillip Seaman warming up for a competition.

Tilt Twisting Mechanics (Figs 18 & 19)

Using hypothetical quantities, if a performer takes off with 100 per cent angular momentum but loses 20 per cent angular momentum by tilting his or her body sideways, then according to the law of conservation of angular momentum, this 20 per cent loss must be regained. This is achieved as the body moves off-centre – when this occurs the body becomes shorter around the somersaulting axis, and the 20 per cent angular momentum is therefore regained.

Tilt twisting in trampolining is used in multiple twisting somersaults and is initiated by arm action. This arm action moves the body off-centre thus creating tilt and it is the degree of this tilt that determines the amount of twist produced. There are several ways in which the arms can be used to produce the desired twist, but some are more efficient than others. To achieve a small amount of twist, the arms are moved out to the sides and rotate through 90 degrees in front of the body (as shown in Fig 18) before being brought in to the body to accelerate the twist. If more twist is required then more tilt must be produced – the arms must move through more of a circle. Fig 19 demonstrates the 'wind up' technique whereby both arms move through a complete circle, initially in the direction opposite to that of the desired twist.

Just as the arms are used to create tilt, they must also be used to square it up when

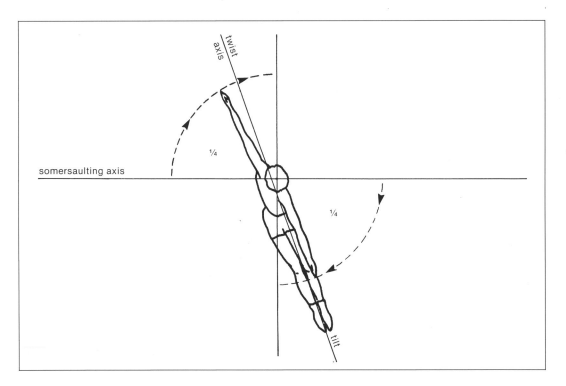

Fig 18 Tilt twisting mechanics.

the required amount of twist has been achieved. It should also be noted that the more angular momentum involved in a move, the faster the twist will be — this is sometimes demonstrated in multiple twisting somersaults such as the rudi-out fliffis. In this case performers may find that they end up doing a randi-out instead, as the twist in the second somersault is much faster than that in the first and the twist in the third somersault is even faster.

It has therefore been proven here that twist in multiple somersaults can be created in mid-air using the above methods without any twist being created from the bed.

Half Twist to Seat Drop and Feet

To perform this move the trampolinist must carry out a half-twist jump with a small amount of forward rotation so that when the half twist is completed the body is leaning back slightly, ready for the legs to be brought up into the seat drop. On landing in the seat drop, the performer must push off with the fingertips as on leaving the trampoline to return to a standing position. For a twist to be incorporated into this move, one shoulder is pulled back and the other brought forward, with the head turned in the direction of the desired twist.

Swivel Hips (Figs 20 – 3)

The full name of this skill is 'seat drop, half twist to seat drop'. The take-off for this move is the same as for the seat drop, but on lifting from the trampoline as when coming to the feet after a seat drop, the performer must sit forwards. If this is not done then the balance and position for

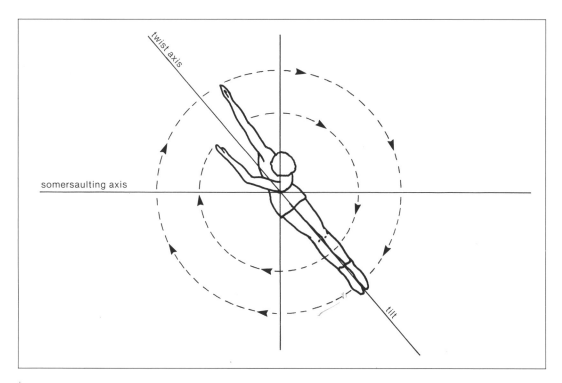

Fig 19   Wind up technique of twisting.

Figs 20 – 3   Swivel hips. Note that during the half twist the body is straight.

Fig 21

Fig 22

Fig 23

the second half twist to the seat is lost and the return to the feet is impossible.

Roller

The full name of this move is 'seat drop, full twist to seat drop'. This is completely different to the swivel hips. In the roller the peformer must sit quite far back while pulling back on one shoulder and forwards on the other. Before starting the twist, the hip angle should be wide. To complete a full twist the performer must bring the arms into his or her sides to accelerate the twist, leaving the arms and hands in the perfect place to resume the seat drop position. This move cannot be performed correctly if the performer does not sit back enough. Another very common fault occurs when the performer starts twisting too early, before leaving the trampoline. This would be apparent at the end of the move because the legs would be pointing to the side instead of straight down the middle as in the first seat drop.

Half Twist to Front Drop, Half Twist to Feet

The take-off for this move is similar to that for the back drop. It needs slightly less rotation than a back drop where the legs rotate 180 degrees from standing. The hips are pushed slightly forwards and upwards and as the performer leaves the trampoline the twist is initiated by pulling the shoulder in the direction of the twist. It is very common for performers learning this move to twist too early which means that they will not land squarely and will also land short because the twist was initiated in place of the rotation.

Once the performer has almost com-

pleted the half twist he can start to prepare for the landing by bending the elbows and knees ready for a front drop. It is quite hard to reach a standing position from a front drop with a half twist, so the landing must be perfect. The chest is pushed up by the arms as the legs are flicked straight. Whilst the arms are pushing, one shoulder is pulled back to initiate the twist. The legs can get in the way if they are flicked straight too early, so the timing is very important — they must flick straight as the performer starts to leave the bed.

Half Twist to Back Drop, Half Twist to Feet (Figs 24 – 8)

The take-off for the half twist to back drop is the same as for that of a front drop, but a little more rotation is needed. As the

Fig 24 – 6   Half twist to back drop.

Fig 25

Fig 26

Figs 27 & 28 Half twist to feet.

performer leaves the trampoline and after the rotation has been created, then one shoulder can be dropped to start the twist. As only a half twist is required, the arms stay out to the sides (if they were brought in to the waist the performer would overtwist). As the performer loses sight of the trampoline then preparation for the back drop landing can begin with the performer bending at the hips. To master the half twist to feet the performer must not twist off the bed. Failing to widen the hip angle as well as twisting straight from the bed causes travel towards the springs at the side of the trampoline.

Beating the feet down gently will return the performer to the standing position. As the body straightens the twist is created, not by the legs but by the hips and torso. It is important in any back drop landing that the legs are slightly short of vertical on landing otherwise it is very hard to keep them in control.

Fig 28

Twisting and Basic Routines

Cradle (Figs 29 – 32)

This move is also called the 'back drop, half twist to back drop'. To get the feel of the amount of rotation needed for this skill the performer should practise some back drops to front drops. As the performer lands in the back drop position the knees can be slightly relaxed (almost bent). As the bed recoils the performer straightens the legs – this helps to maintain the height whilst creating rotation. Almost double the rotation is needed than is required for the back drop to feet. If the performer is short of rotation when first learning the move then piking a little or even tucking will speed the rotation up a little. Figs 29 – 32 show the sequence of manoeuvres for the cradle: Fig 29 shows the slight knee bend before leaving the bed; Fig 30 shows the flight in the air before the twist; Fig 31 shows the body position (straight) during the twist; and Fig 32 shows the landing in the back drop position.

Once the back drop to front drop has been mastered, the performer can start to put in the half twist as soon as the trampoline comes into sight. The twist is initiated in the usual way by pulling back on one shoulder and forward with the other. The arms stay out to the sides when learning this move and the twist must not be created off the trampoline otherwise the performer will be short of rotation. After the half twist the performer prepares for the back drop landing which is the same as for the ordinary half twist to back.

Figs 29 – 32 Sequence of manoeuvres for the cradle.

Fig 30

Back Bouncing (Figs 33 & 34)

Although this is not a twist manoeuvre, it is a good idea to master back bouncing before moving on to the more difficult twist moves. Back bouncing is a very difficult skill, but once mastered it opens up the ability to learn even more difficult skills with greater ease.

When landing on the back in preparation for back bouncing, the angle between the hips and thighs must never exceed ninety degrees. It may be slightly less, but if it is even a fraction over ninety degrees, performers will find themselves returning to the feet or to a seat drop. Once the performer has landed in the correct position with the knees slightly bent (as discussed in the cradle), the performer

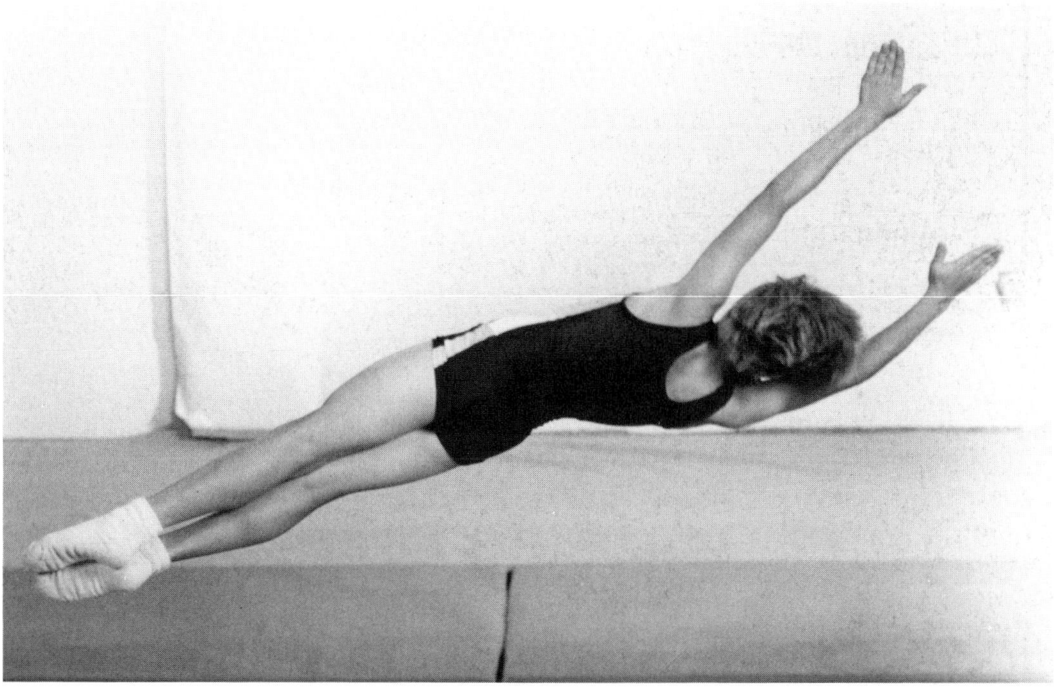

Fig 31

Fig 32

Fig 33   The knee bend which is required during back bouncing.

Fig 34 *The correct angle of the body between back bounces.*

must then kick both upwards and slightly backwards. In between each back bounce the performer may extend the body, pushing the hips up before returning to the back drop position. Back bouncing is very difficult to learn and has a lot to do with timing the knee bend and knee kick — this only comes with practice.

Back Drop, Full Twist to Back Drop (Figs 35 – 8)

If a cat is held upside-down (with its back parallel to the floor) and is then let go, it will always land on its feet (providing it is dropped from sufficient height in which to complete a half twist). This is consequently known as the 'cat twist' and can be used quite often by performers in trampolining. The back drop, full twist to back drop is one of the moves in which the cat twist is used.

After landing in a back drop and kicking upwards and backwards as in back bounc-ing, the performer straightens the body in preparation for the twist. One shoulder is pulled back as the hips turn in the desired direction of twist. The head and opposite shoulder follow this direction and the arms are brought in to the body to accelerate the twist slightly. When the full twist is almost complete the arms are brought out from the side again to slow the twist down and the body is piked in preparation for the back drop landing. The twist is only a cat twist if it is initiated in the air — if the performer starts twisting from the trampoline bed it is not a cat twist, and the performer will also travel too close to the side of the trampoline during the twist.

Mechanics of the Cat Twist (Fig 39)

Fig 39 shows the piked position which can be used to initiate the action/reaction twist (the arch can also be used). When the body

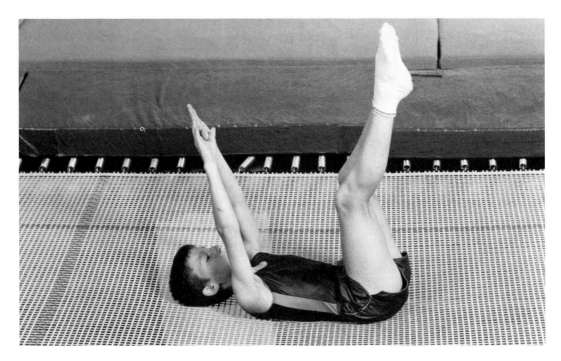

Fig 35−8   Back drop followed by full twist to back drop.

Fig 36

Fig 37

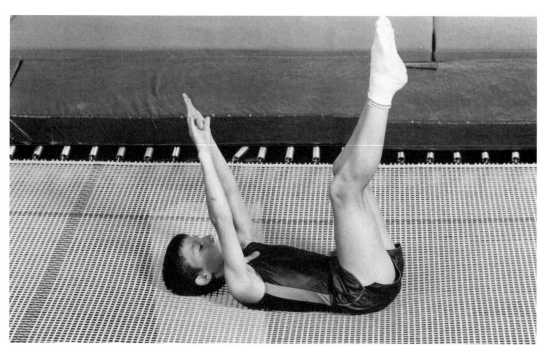

Fig 38

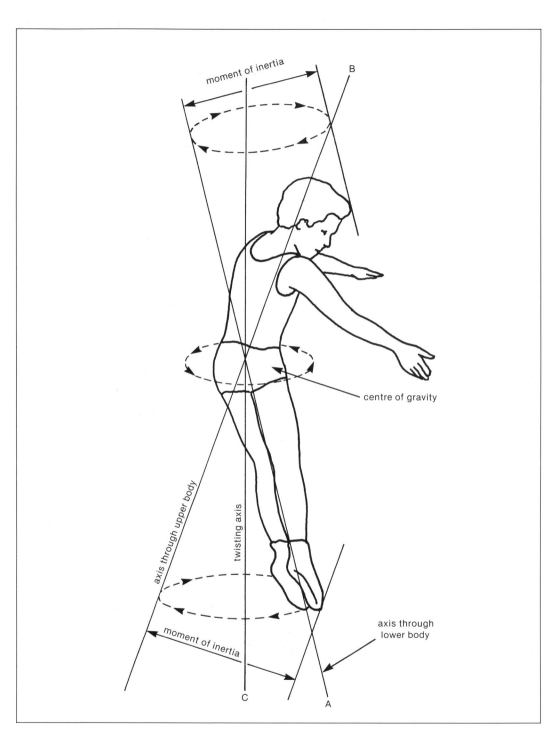

Fig 39   Mechanics of the cat twist.

is in this position, the axes through the upper and the lower body cross. The upper body can then twist against the moment of inertia of the legs, followed by the legs twisting against the moment of inertia of the upper body. By repeating this action, the performer's body will twist around Axis C without any twist being created from the trampoline bed. The action/reaction of the trunk is seen by a conical swinging of the legs while the leg action/reaction is seen by a similar movement of the trunk.

ROUTINES

Trampolining is all about routines. A routine consists of linking together various skills without free bounces between moves. Enough skills have now been learned to put together some basic routines. It is important to remember that in a routine the landing from one move is the take-off for another. Perfect landings therefore mean perfect take-offs, just as a bad landing from one move may lead to a bad take-off for the following move. If the latter occurs it may possibly result in the end of the routine.

A competitive routine consists of ten different movements linked together. The best way to build routines for competition is discussed later, in Chapter 8. Meanwhile, mastering routines which include the skills covered so far will enhance the performer's awareness of linking routines and also the problems that can arise from incorrect technique.

Routine 1

1. Front drop
2. Return to feet
3. Straddle jump
4. Half-twist jump
5. Seat drop
6. Half twist to seat drop
7. Half twist to feet
8. Tuck jump
9. Pike jump
10. Full-twist jump

Routine 2

1. Full-twist jump
2. Straddle jump
3. Seat drop
4. Half twist to seat drop
5. Half twist to feet
6. Pike jump
7. Back drop
8. Half twist to feet
9. Tuck jump
10. Half-twist jump

Routine 3

1. Back drop
2. Cradle (half twist to back drop)
3. Half twist to feet
4. Straddle jump
5. Full-twist jump
6. Tuck jump
7. Half twist to seat drop
8. Half twist to feet
9. Pike jump
10. Half-twist jump

4 Basic Somersaulting and Advanced Routines

BASIC SOMERSAULTS

Forward Rotation

This is usually the first direction in which the performer learns to somersault. There is less fear involved in rotating forwards for the beginner. Later on however, peformers usually prefer to rotate backwards because the bed can be seen as the performer comes to land (in the front turnover or somersault the landing is called a 'blind' landing as the bed cannot be seen).

Mechanics of Forward Rotation (Fig 41) — Points to Remember

1.   The speed of the throw is very important — the faster the upper body is moved,

the earlier the performer can block, thus more height will be achieved.
2.   The block should occur when the bed is fully recoiled and when the legs have reached their full extension. This will give maximum eccentric thrust (hip drive).
3.   A common mistake occurs when performers start to throw the upper body to initiate the rotation as they are dropping on to the bed. This causes the hips, shoulders and feet to move out of line and reduces the amount of power produced. It results in the performer sitting the move as the hips have moved backwards.
4.   When throwing the head, shoulders and arms to initiate the rotation, it is very important that performers keep the arms close together. If the arms are wide when throwing, the distance from the fingertips to

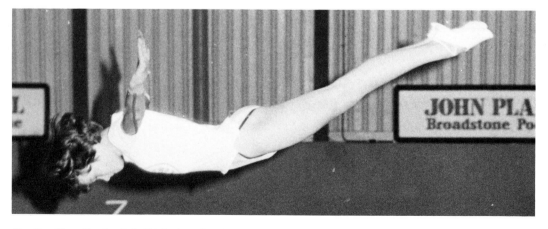

Fig 40   Clare Haydon (née Fricker) performing a crash dive.

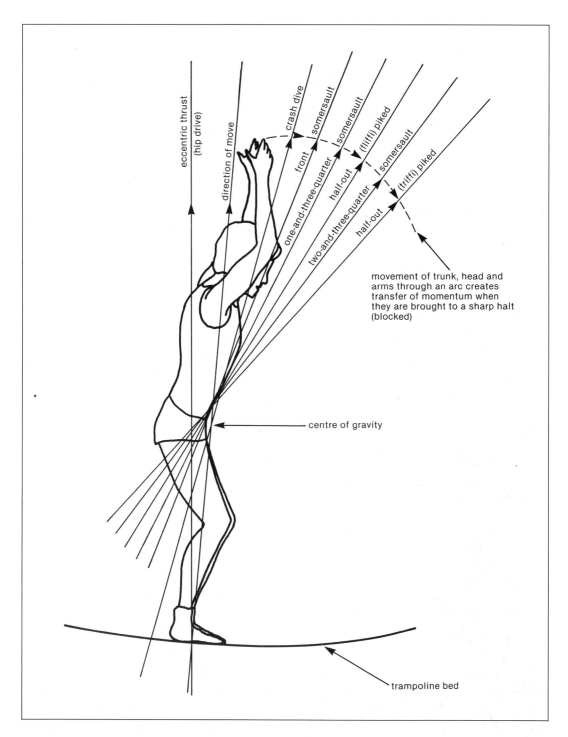

Fig 41   Mechanics of forward rotation.

the hips is less than if they were kept close together so when the arms are thrown downwards, less leverage is available and less rotation will be produced.

5.   Effective blocking will eliminate excess centrifugal force and so the body shape when rotating will be tight, whether the body is in a tucked or piked position.

6.   If a performer has long, heavy legs and a slight upper body he or she wil rotate badly. As the rotation is produced by throwing and then blocking the upper body, if this part of the body is proportionally smaller then the transfer of momentum will be less effective. Performers with this problem can overcome it to a certain extent by carrying out high weight, low repetition weighttraining. This will build up the upper body so that it is more in proportion, however it is not advisable for trampolinists under 14 years old.

7.   Conversely, performers with short legs and larger bodies will somersault well, but they will not be able to twist as effectively.

Hands and Knees
Drop, Forward Turnover

This work-up is usually used simply to get the performer used to rotating upsidedown. The trampolinist performs a hands and knees drop but, on landing, instead of pushing up to the feet or extending out into a front drop, the legs are extended whilst the hips are pushed up and the head and torso dropped. This will usually bring the performer round to either a back drop or a seat drop position. It is a good idea for the coach to push a crash mat onto the trampoline in time for the landing because in the early stages the performer tends to land in between a seat drop and a back drop which can be quite uncomfortable. The controlled hands and knees forward turnover to back

drop and return to feet, and the same to seat drop and up to feet should be mastered as this skill is one of the moves needed to pass the BTF Trampoline Proficiency Badges.

Rotation from the feet can be included now. Figs 42 − 4 show the hands and knees forward turnover to seat. It can either be carried out in the open piked position as shown or can be performed in a tucked position with an extension before the landing.

Front Somersault

As mentioned, the best way to let the performer gain experience of the somersault take-off is to place a crash mat on the trampoline. The performer bounces at one end of the trampoline with the arms above the head and on a balanced bounce throws the arms downwards, pushing the hips up and tucking the head under. The performer is usually quite confident about attempting this having already experienced the rotation of a turnover from the hands and knees. The crash mat tends to kill the bounce but this in itself is quite convenient in the early stages as the performer will not have the added worry of over-rotating.

The performer should be careful not to twist on take-off − even a slight twist can take years to correct if it is not noticed early enough. Always concentrate on throwing the arms closely down the middle. Once the take-off is looking more confident and the performer feels safe, the crash mat can be removed and the somersault take-off can be performed on its own with the coach standing in and catching the performer on landing. Alternatively the overhead spotting rig could be used but this tends to restrict the performer's movement, apart from the fact that not every hall has one.

Fig 42–4   Hands and knees forward turnover to seat

Now that the progressions of the forward somersault have been discussed, the following outlines what the end product should look like. The performer should always start the somersault take-off with the arms above the head. This is because in a routine the arms always reach above the head between each move. This does not mean that the performer has to carry out all the pre-bouncing with the arms above the head — when the trampolinist is ready to perform the move the arms are kept above the head for the bounce before the somersault. The performer must throw the arms up and over rather than downwards as this provides both height and rotation. The hips are pushed back a little and the required position is assumed. The beginner will initially perform a front somersault in a tucked position (see Figs 45–8), before progressing to the piked or straight front somersault. These positions are held for about three quarters of the somersault

Fig 43

39

Fig 44

Fig 45 Throwing the arms in an 'up and over' action.

Fig 46 Taking up the tucked position.

Fig 47 & 48   The line-out before landing.

Fig 48

before the performer opens out into a straight line, with the arms tight by the sides. This is called the 'line-out' and in order to gain good marks in a competition all skills should be lined out, showing good judgement of rotation.

In a piked front somersault the technique is the same as for the tucked front somersault. The performer takes off as shown in Fig 45, however the arms must be thrown up and over more sharply to create slightly more hip lift. The body, as has already been shown, rotates slower in the piked position than in the tucked position − this is why more rotation is needed on take-off for a piked front somersault.

Forward Somersault Straight

The forward somersault straight is rarely used in a routine. It is a difficult skill to master, but is a very good work-up for many moves. The reason it is such a difficult manoeuvre is because the correct amount of rotation must be created on take-off. Unlike the tucked and piked front somersaults where the performer can adjust if the take-off is slightly wrong (by pulling in the tuck or pike or lining out either earlier or later), there is no adjustment that can be made in a front somersault straight because the performer is lined out from the beginning. This is the reason it is rarely used in competition routines − it is considered to have the same degree of difficulty as the piked front somersault but is in reality a great deal harder to perform.

However, as mentioned above, the move is a very good work-up for forward somersaults with twists. A lot more rotation is needed for a straight front somersault than for the tucked and piked somersaults, just as a lot more rotation is needed for a front somersault with either half, one-and-a-half

or two-and-a-half twists. Thus, before learning to twist in a front somersault it is a good idea to feel the amount of rotation needed for the move by practising some front somersaults straight. The coach may wish to push a crash mat on the bed for the move because the performer will always initially under-rotate. The throw of the arms on take-off is much more vigorous in this move and the hips are pushed back more whilst the heels drive upwards. As the performer leaves the bed the arms are brought into the sides. The performer will probably have to break form at the end of the first few practice somersaults before the courage to create the amount of rotation needed has been gained. As the performer appears to be getting the idea of the amount of rotation needed, the coach should stand in at the end of the somersault in case the performer over-rotates.

Backward Rotation

The Mechanics of Backward Rotation (*Fig 49*) − Points to Remember

The backward rotation here refers to that in a first move, as opposed to backward rotation during swingtime.

1. The speed that the arms move past the hips and upwards past the trunk is very important as it is this action which causes the bed to depress further than it would by body-weight alone (through action/reaction). The arms should not bend too much as power will be lost.

2. The performer should block the arms (*see* Glossary) before allowing the body to start moving backwards. The head, trunk and arms are then moved together backwards in an arc (*see* Fig 49) − the amount

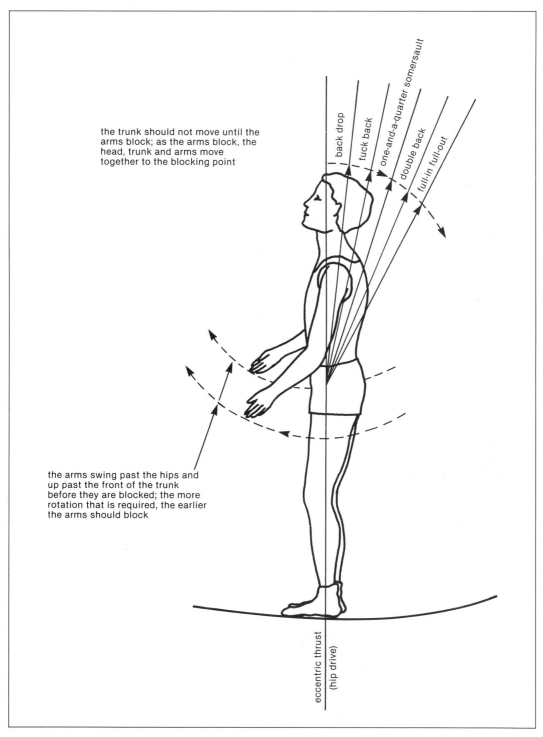

the trunk should not move until the arms block; as the arms block, the head, trunk and arms move together to the blocking point

back drop

tuck back

one-and-a-quarter somersault

double back

full-in full-out

the arms swing past the hips and up past the front of the trunk before they are blocked; the more rotation that is required, the earlier the arms should block

eccentric thrust (hip drive)

Fig 49   Mechanics of backward rotation

Figs 50–3 Back drop, back pullover.

Fig 51 The legs are pulled over the head to perform the back pullover.

Fig 52

of movement depends upon the move which is being performed. The upper body then blocks and the body shape at this stage is perfect for eccentric thrust (hip lift).

3. Many world-class performers start moves involving backwards rotation with their arms above their heads thereby missing out the upward arm swing completely. By doing this a certain amount of bed depression is lost, but as the arms are above the head, the leverage of the throwing arc becomes greater and rotation is more easily created. Performers should use the technique that suits them best. Omitting the arm swing however, requires good shoulder mobility as the arms must be held directly above the head without the lower back muscles loosening. If a performer has stiff shoulders it is therefore advisable that they opt for the arm swing, or if he or she has good shoulder mobility the

alternative technique can be used — they are both mechanically sound.

Back Drop, Back Pullover (Figs 50–3)

The pullover (as it is known) from a back drop is usually the first way a performer feels backward rotation to any degree. Some learn this move without being taught it — simply by experimenting on their own. Other more careful or less confident performers prefer to wait until they are taught.

To achieve the pullover the performer must first land in a good back drop position with the legs vertical, the arms parallel with the legs and the head on the trampoline bed. As the bed depresses the legs are brought over the face (see Fig 50) giving more of a piked position. As the performer leaves the trampoline the position of the body should stay piked until the performer has turned over and has seen the trampoline below. Then the body can straighten out. It is important that the performer stays in a piked position in order to keep rotating. With repetition the performer will feel that the body can be straightened earlier, but the initial rotation must have been created by pulling over with the legs.

Backward Somersaults

The first backward somersault learned by a trampolinist is the backward somersault tucked. One of the best ways in which to learn this move is for the coach to hold the back of the performer's leotard or shorts and to bounce with the performer. On the count of three the performer must quickly swing the arms up above the head and then stop this motion sharply to create the necessary rotation. Then the performer

Fig 53

must bring the knees into the chest and tuck with one hand on each shin.

It is very common for trampolinists learning this move to swing the arms up and stop them but to forget to tuck, or to concentrate so much on tucking that they forget to swing the arms up. Coaches must therefore be very aware that in these first attempts at a backward somersault they may well be doing more work than the performer. If the performer is young and quite light this is not such a problem, however if the performer is older and heavy the coach may well need the additional help of someone pushing in the crash mat. If two coaches are available in this case it is also a good idea to have each one bouncing on either side of the heavier performer. Whether one or two coaches are available their job is the same: as the performer takes off and usually on the count of three, the coach places one hand on the performer's lower back to assist the hip lift with the other hand guiding the performer's arms above the head at the right speed and position. The coach must

Fig 54   The coach supporting a performer for a backwards somersault tucked.

hold the performer throughout the somersault until he or she is confident of the landing. It would be a waste of time for a performer to be assisted on take-off and then left to land in a heap. As performers become more confident then they may well be left to land on their own but this is inadvisable in the very early stages. Alternatively an overhead spotting rig may be used if one is available.

After performers have successfully completed many backward somersaults under the guidance of the coach and are being assisted only slightly then they should be ready to do the move on their own (with the coach standing in after take-off). The coach stands on the side of the trampoline and as the performer leaves the trampoline the coach can step in (without killing the performer's bounce) and assist with the hip lift by giving a little push to the performer's lower back. (This would only be necessary however, if the coach saw that the performer had not created enough rotation on take-off.) Then, as the performer opens out of the tuck, the coach puts one hand on the performer's chest and the other on the performer's back to help with stability on landing. As the move becomes more consistent the coach can gradually leave the performer to take off and land on his or her own.

A backward somersault should not travel back too much. Performers must ensure that they do not jump their feet forwards on take-off — this will make the body tilt backwards, creating uncontrollable rotation without height. The rotation that is needed is created by swinging the arms quickly and closely past the waist, up to the line of the ears. It is important that the head is held in line with the body. If the head is held right back, the arms would have to travel much further back to reach the ear-line and thus too much rotation would be created. The tucked or piked position must be assumed quite quickly and smoothly so that plenty of time is left for a straight line-out before landing.

The piked backward somersault (*see* Figs 55 – 7) can be executed with performers either touching their toes or holding their arms behind the knees. Touching the toes is becoming increasingly popular in single somersaults, however, if the trampolinist wishes to hold the arms behind the knees it is tidier if the elbows are kept in at the sides. With either method the knees must be straight and a good pike must be shown with the head following the line of the body.

Fig 55 – 7   The take-off, piked position and line-out of the piked backward somersault.

Fig 56

Back Somersault Straight (Figs 58 – 60)

Unlike the front somersault straight, the back somersault straight is used frequently in routines and as a work-up. It is difficult to master, needing much more rotation than the tucked or piked back somersaults, but because performers can see where they are going throughout the straight back (unlike the front somersault, which has a completely blind landing) not so much fear is involved in learning this manoeuvre. The straight back again demands the performer to move the arms very fast and stop them before the line of the ears. The shoulders are pulled back a very small amount (compared to the tucked and piked back where they are not pulled back at all). When the arms have been stopped, they are brought

Fig 57

Fig 58   The 'block' on take-off and the hip lift during the back somersault straight.

back to the sides and held there throughout the somersault. As the arms are brought down to the sides the hips are lifted up. Much more hip lift is needed in a straight back than in a tucked or piked back. Stopping the arms before take-off is known as 'blocking' the arms and is only efficient if tension is maintained in the upper abdominal and dorsal back areas.

When learning the straight back, performers tend to take some time in mastering the amount of rotation needed to cause the body to pike during the move. Either performers do not block early enough, the arms are brought up too slowly, or they do not produce the amount of hip lift required. Again, performers should be careful not to let the head pull back on take-off. Pulling the head back on take-off in any move is a very difficult habit to break and is either the result of an under-rotated take-off or anxiety.

Figs 59 & 60   The line-out throughout the back somersault straight.

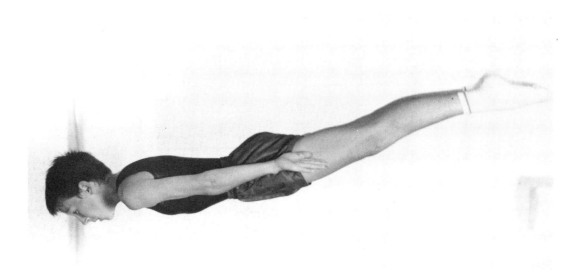

Fig 60

Back Somersault to Seat

This move, along with the one-and-a-quarter back somersault to back drop, are two moves that performers often use in their earlier years of trampolining, to increase the overall difficulty of their routines. However, when a performer becomes more competent with an increased vocabulary of moves, it is not usually necessary to use these manoeuvres in voluntary routines. They are part of the compulsory routines however, so it is necessary for the performer to master them.

The back somersault to seat drop is very straightforward to learn. Coaches are advised to push a crash mat in for the first few attempts — more than anything to kill the bounce after the seat drop. The performer should by now be quite a good judge of rotation and it should take only a few efforts for him or her to feel the slight amount of extra rotation this move needs compared to the tuck back. It is probably fair to say that the tucked back somersault to seat needs about the same amount of rotation as the pike back. The move is the same as the tuck back with a straight line-out, however instead of landing on the feet, the performer prepares for a seat drop with the fingers pointing forwards. When performers first attempt the move without a crash mat, the coach should stand in to catch them after the seat drop. This is because if performers were to over-rotate the tuck back to seat with their heels landing after their hips they may 'kaboom' onto their necks. They also may under-rotate the move and in this case, instead of coming up to their feet, they would go past their feet. The latter is not so worrying, however, because a performer could move to either a front drop or swivel hips. It is advisable that a coach is present to assist, in case the performer does not think quickly enough to correct any mistake. An experienced coach will be aware of the common faults that occur when learning any skills, but the inexperienced coach should always be particularly alert when teaching a move for the first time.

The usual recovery from a back somersault to seat is a half twist to the feet.

One-and-a-quarter Back Somersault to Back Drop (Figs 61–6)

As previously mentioned, the tuck back to seat has about the same amount of rotation as the pike back. The one-and-a-quarter tuck back to back however, has approximately the same amount of rotation as the straight back. In the first few attempts, performers will probably be short of rotation so it is again advisable for the coach to push a crash mat in to eliminate discomfort on landing as well as to kill the bounce as

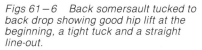

Figs 61–6 Back somersault tucked to back drop showing good hip lift at the beginning, a tight tuck and a straight line-out.

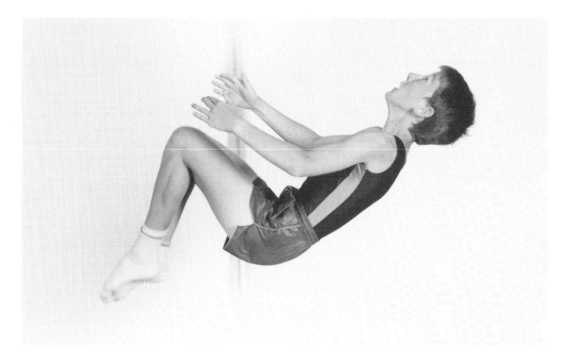

Fig 62

Fig 63

Fig 64

the performer lands on the back. Performers generally will not want to think about a line-out when learning this move, and will just stay tucked before opening straight into a back drop position – it is later, after gaining more rotation and more control that they can experiment with a line-out.

Again, when the performer first attempts this move without the crash mat, a coach should stand in to assist in whichever landing is chosen following the back drop. A pullover is very easy from a one-and-a-quarter back because sufficient momentum has already been gathered when coming into the bed and only the additional pull of the legs is required for the performer to return to the feet.

A back pullover should never be attempted from an under-rotated one-and-a-quarter back.

Fig 65

Fig 66

Crash Dive (Figs 67 – 71)

This is a straight three-quarter forward somersault with the performer taking off as in a front somersault, except with less hip lift. When leaving the bed the performer should push right up above the head, lifting the heels up behind. The arms spread out to the side after the extension from the trampoline and the body is kept in a straight position for about half of the somersault. When the body is vertical above the trampoline the performer should start to prepare for the landing by slowly piking under. If the pike under (also called a 'duck under') is too fast the legs will move back and the rotation will become too fast.

When first learning to crash dive performers should place a crash mat on the trampoline. By simply practising a forward turnover onto the back the performer can

Figs 67 – 71 Crash dive.

Figs 68

Fig 69

learn the skill and progress by gradually opening out into a straight position and introducing more heel lift as confidence increases. When the performer eventually takes the crash mat away, a coach should stand in at the end of the skill as the performer returns to the feet or carries out a half twist to feet. It is vitally important for performers to remember that the head must be on the trampoline when landing in a back drop position.

Lazy Back

This manoeuvre consists of a straight three-quarter back somersault, landing in a front drop. The take-off for this move is the same as for the back somersault straight except less rotation is needed. The arms should initially block and then return to the sides quickly in order for a straight line-out position to be reached before the performer prepares for the landing. The landing

Fig 70

Fig 71

preparation begins just after the half somersault has been executed, where a 180 degree rotation has been achieved. At this time the performer has a clear sight of the bed. The arms are now brought away from the sides and are bent, along with the knees, ready for the front drop landing. Again this move should first be practised on a crash mat or with the use of a spotting rig, as bad judgement of rotation during this move can result in a performer injuring his or her back.

SWINGTIME *(Figs 72 – 7)*

Linking together two or more movements is called 'swingtime'. At the end of Chapter 3 a few beginner's routines were covered. A few more advanced routines, including the somersaults recently covered are given below, but first the correct technique for linking together somersaults must be learned.

Figs 72 – 7   Swingtime.

Fig 73

Figs 76 and 77 show the correct action for the landing from one back somersault into the take-off for another. As the performer finishes the line-out of a back somersault and prepares to land, the arms should lift up so that they are straight out in front of the performer and continue moving upwards on landing ready for the next skill. If the arms are too low, or are not moving upwards on landing, then the force of the landing will make them feel too heavy to lift. As the bed reaches maximum depression, the performer should be swinging the arms up and on leaving the bed the performer should be blocking the arms (*see* Glossary for a definition). If the performer lands with the arms too high then one of two things may happen. Either:

1. The performer will overreach because without some arm movement insufficient rotation will be produced. However, overreaching will cause less height and

Fig 74

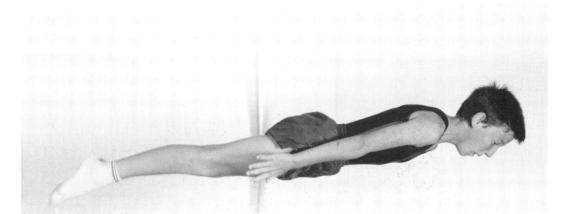

Fig 75

body tension and too much uncontrolled rotation; or,

2. If the performer does not move the arms because they were in the correct place to block on landing, then insufficient rotation will be produced again.

Timing is therefore vitally important in linking together somersaults in order to gain and not lose height during routines. The same technique occurs in linking back somersaults and front somersaults, except that instead of stopping the movement of the arms as they reach above the head, they are brought up above the head and are pushed up and over for the front somersault. The arms should never swing past the waist when linking together either front or back somersaults as they would when linking together tuck, pike and straddle jumps.

Fig 76

Fig 77

MORE ADVANCED ROUTINES

Routine 1

1. Tucked back somersault
2. Seat drop
3. Half twist to feet
4. Full-twist jump
5. Straddle jump
6. Back drop
7. Half twist to feet
8. Half-twist jump
9. Tuck jump
10. Front somersault tucked

Routine 2

1. Crash dive
2. Half twist to feet
3. Tuck jump
4. Tuck back
5. Tuck back to seat
6. Half twist to feet
7. Straddle jump
8. Pike back
9. Pike jump
10. Pike front

It is also important that the performer comes in from each back somersault with the body-weight slightly over the toes, so that by the time the bed is depressed the body will be upright. Performers who are very powerful need to come in from each somersault with their weight further forward than performers who gain less height. This is because the trampoline bed depresses more the higher a performer bounces.

5 Advanced Twisting

Somersaults with Twists

Barani (Figs 79−83)

This is a front somersault with a half twist and can be done in any of the three positions (tucked, piked or straight). Some trampolinists may use all three shaped baranis in a routine if they are desperate to increase the difficulty factor, but do not have a great vocabulary of moves. However, the performers will usually only do one barani in a routine, especially if it is a compulsory routine − this is usually the straight barani.

It is extremely important that performers learn that they must not twist off the trampoline bed for the barani. If the twist is initiated too soon then the performer will be cast to the side of the trampoline bed and will be short of rotation (or turn). 'Turn before twist' is the rule for any twisting somersault. To emphasise this the barani is always taught with a slight pike and a late half twist. The aim of introducing a pike is to get the performer used to hip lift. Whilst in a piked position it is also hard to twist, so the performer has to open out of the pike before twisting − thus making it impossible to twist off the mat. This introduction of the

Figs 78   Helen Channon performing a straddle jump in competition.

Figs 79–83   Barani.

pike encourages a square barani and eventually the body can be straightened out and the twist brought in earlier to the middle of the somersault.

When learning the barani the trampolinist initially performs a forward somersault open piked with an early extension. When this has been performed successfully, the coach can either stand in or push a crash mat in (or both) after the take-off and call out 'twist'. It is a good idea for the coach to trick the performer after every few attempts by not calling out 'twist', to see if the performer is actually doing an ariel twist. (The twist must be called immediately after take-off and not later.) If the twist is brought in too early then the performer should go back to forward somersaults open piked and start the progression again. It will take a long time for a performer to learn a square barani, so patience is

Fig 80

Fig 81

Fig 82

Fig 83

important. If the performer moves on to other skills too soon it will only mean having to go back to the basics later on. There are no short cuts, and learning good technique early on is vital if more complicated skills are to be added to the performer's vocabulary — bad technique in basic skills would eventually hinder progression.

When the performer has mastered the square barani (which will be executed with a slightly piked position still, with the arms above the head) and has been doing them in routines for a few months, then the man-oeuvre can be straightened out. After straightening it out the performer can then start to bring the arms in to the sides. When first trying the move with the arms by the sides the performer may overtwist a little because the twist is accelerated if the arms are brought in. The arms must therefore be very close on take-off, with the shoulders and arms initiating the twist

soon after the performer leaves the bed.

The performer can see the trampoline bed throughout the barani. Although the take-off for the barani is forwards, the landing is like that of a back somersault, therefore when following this move with another move (such as a back somersault) the technique is the same as discussed in Swingtime (*see* Chapter 4).

Rudi (Rudolph)

This manoeuvre consists of a forward somersault with one-and-a-half twists, the technique being similar to that for a barani. However, being in a rudi the arms are thrown closely for rotation and are then brought out to the sides. As the heels lift during the take-off, the performer 'wraps' in the twist — pulls back with one arm and forwards with the other and then brings both arms in to the chest or by the sides to accelerate the twist. When the one-and-a-half twist has been completed, the arms are again brought out to the sides in order to stop the twist. Obviously it is important to create the right amount of twist on take-off. If too much twist is created then the performer should bring the arms out after the one-and-a-half twist to slow it down (this will not stop it completely, however, and the landing will be unsquare and uncontrolled). Alternatively, if insufficient twist is produced in the early stages the performer may land before the twist has been completed — the more the arms are wrapped before they are brought in, the faster the twist will be. The body and head must also be completely straight and in line throughout the twist. Not only does this look better but the body twists faster when it is in a perfectly straight line.

Back Somersault Straight with a Full Twist (Figs 84 – 8)

The half twisting backward somersault straight is the first backward twisting somersault learned by a trampolinist. The performer is not taught how to execute the manoeuvre straight off with the arms by the sides — as with the barani; this move should be learned by initially doing a late twist, bringing the arms into the chest.

Firstly the performer should practise some straight back somersaults with a good block (i.e. the arms stopping suddenly) and with both arms out to the sides. The arms should be kept close to the body until the performer has blocked and left the bed. When this has been mastered with plenty of rotation being produced, the performer can then try to pull back a little on one arm and forwards on the other. The correct time to start this twist is as soon as the performer

spots the bed — this is about 200 degrees after the half somersault point. It will probably take a performer weeks to be able to complete a full twist. For safety a crash mat should be pushed in for the landing. A common fault is for performers to pull back with the shoulders instead of blocking. When this happens performers usually feel out of control and either do not complete the twist, or if they do, they will probably land on their backs. It is therefore advisable for the coach to be available to catch the performer at the end of the move. This will make for a more comfortable landing and will give the performer added confidence.

Once the performer can complete the full twist every time then work can be done to

Figs 84 – 8   Back somersault straight with a full twist. The twist is initiated by pulling back on one shoulder and speeds up as the arms are brought in to the sides.

Fig 85

Fig 86

improve the actual form of the move. At this stage the twist starts and finishes late, thus leaving no time at the end for the performer to prepare for a good landing. The twist therefore, can gradually be brought in earlier provided the performer is careful not to initiate it before leaving the bed. The twist should not be too fast as this does not look tidy. It should last for most of the somersault, finishing with enough time for the performer to prepare for a good, controlled landing and with the arms preparing for the take-off into the next move. If the twist is completed too early there is more time to break form at the end of the move and the arms will need to be tidied up. The arms should remain next to the sides throughout the twist, so the performer must take off with less twist before bringing the arms by the sides — if not, overtwisting will occur. The arms should block and then be brought into the sides as in the straight

Fig 87

back, but with the performer pulling back slightly on one shoulder and bringing the other forwards.

Double Full

This consists of a straight back somersault with a double twist and the performer who is ready to learn this move will have been completing full twisting backs in routines for at least a year. Again, it is easier initially for a performer to learn the double full with the arms folded across the chest. In fact not many trampolinists perform the double full with the arms by their sides, because it takes a very accurate take-off to master the technique — if mastered correctly however, it looks terrific.

The performer learning the double full should return to practising a full with wider

Fig 88

arms that are brought in to the chest. The crash mat should be pushed in for the landing from the full. As the performer sees the bed after completing the full twist he or she can keep the arms in to the chest to continue twisting, rather than preparing to land by bringing the arms away from the chest. It is quite common for performers to have to do the one-and-a-half twisting back somersault a few times before they have the confidence to keep their arms in to their chest which is necessary to complete the double twist. Once performers have completed their first double twisting back somersault it is very common that they may regress slightly and may not even be able to complete the one-and-a-half twist. This is because the double twisting back can be quite a frightening experience at first with performers not knowing where they are in relation to the trampoline during somersaulting and twisting. Also, because the twist is executed much more slowly when the move is being learned, performers feel as if they are twisting forever. However, given time, performers will soon be able to tell where they are in the air (this is called aerial awareness) and will be completing the double twist more often. Soon the twist will become tidier and faster and the performer will have enough time before landing to prepare the arms and body for the take-off into another move.

Randi (Randolph) and Triple Full

The randi is a two-and-a-half twisting front somersault while the triple full is a back somersault with three twists. In the same way as progressing from a rudi to a double full has been described, so the randi and triple full can be learned. The wider and more vigorous the wrap before the arms are brought in, the more twist is created. For a randi or triple full the arms should wrap wide for nearly a complete twist before being brought into the chest.

When twisting forward in trampolining, twists are in halves: barani — half twisting front somersault; rudi — one-and-a-half twisting front somersault; randi — two-and-a-half twisting front somersault. However, when twisting backwards twists are complete: full; double full; triple full. This is so the performer can spot the bed on all of the landings, whether the move consists of a forward or backward take-off. Being able to spot the trampoline at the end of a move makes it much easier and safer to link moves together.

6 Advanced Combinations and Competitions

ADVANCED COMBINATIONS

Ball-out

After mastering the crash dive and before going on to the one-and-three-quarter front

Fig 89 Mandy Phelps performing a pike back drop.

somersault the performer must learn to complete a ball-out. This is a forward somersault from the back drop landing position. Primarily performers should learn a ball-out front somersault to feet, which is a one-and-a-quarter somersault from the back drop all the way round to the feet. It is always learned from a crash dive rather than an ordinary back drop because the crash dive already produces sufficient forward momentum when the performer is coming into the trampoline bed for him or her to be carried forward into the ball-out. In Back Bouncing (see Chapter 3) the knee bend and knee kick were discussed and it is in the ball-out that the full benefit of a well-timed knee kick is felt (see Figs 91 – 4).

The first progression to be learned is called a 'bounce roll' and is a forward somersault from a back drop round to a back drop. The crash mat should be pushed in for this as with most new moves. It will take many attempts before this move is successfully mastered with the necessary height and control and without too much travel; in fact, the performer will probably be able to safely complete a ball-out front before mastering a bounce roll without the crash mat. Performers may, when first attempting the bounce roll, turn right around to land on their seat in fear of landing on their head — it is fine for performers to bypass the bounce roll temporarily as long as they master it

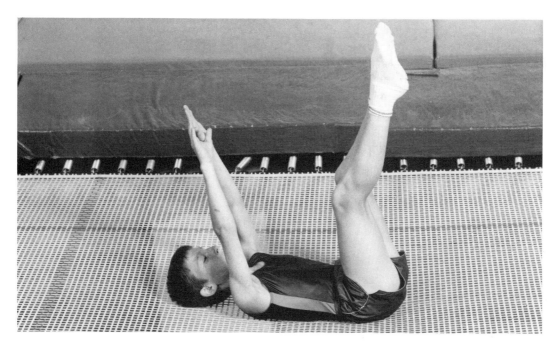

Figs 90–3   The knee bend and knee kick needed for a high controlled
bounce roll.

Fig 91

Fig 92

Fig 93

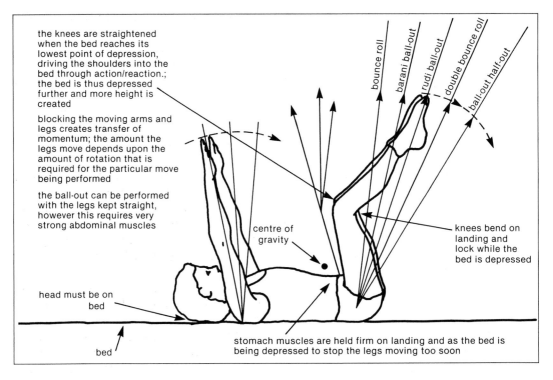

the knees are straightened when the bed reaches its lowest point of depression, driving the shoulders into the bed through action/reaction.; the bed is thus depressed further and more height is created

blocking the moving arms and legs creates transfer of momentum; the amount the legs move depends upon the amount of rotation that is required for the particular move being performed

the ball-out can be performed with the legs kept straight, however this requires very strong abdominal muscles

bounce roll

barani ball-out

rudi ball-out

double bounce roll

ball-out half-out

centre of gravity

knees bend on landing and lock while the bed is depressed

head must be on bed

bed

stomach muscles are held firm on landing and as the bed is being depressed to stop the legs moving too soon

Fig 94   Mechanics of the ball-out.

eventually. If performers can do several bounce rolls linked together while maintaining the height and without a great deal of travel then they will undoubtedly be able to perform successful ball-outs with many variations. However, the ball-out front somersault to feet is simply a matter of completing numerous repetitions until the performer becomes more confident and controlled — just as when he or she was learning the ordinary front somersault. As well as pushing in the crash mat, the coach can stand in at the end of the move to help the performer complete a controlled landing.

The ball-out front somersault is rarely, if ever, used in routines because it has a blind landing. However, the ball-out barani and ball-out rudi are frequently used in routines and once mastered are easier and safer for the trampolinist to perform. The ball-out barani can be learned as soon as the ball-out front somersault can be completed safely. There is not really any need for a performer to be able to complete a ball-out front off the crash mat before learning the ball-out barani.

The ball-out barani is nearly always initially learned in the tucked position and as the performer should by this stage be familiar with tucked, piked and straight baranis, aerial awareness of the ball-out barani should come very quickly. A common fault however, is for the performer to start twisting too early, therefore losing sight of the bed — the bed must be spotted before the performer starts to twist.

Mechanics of the Ball-out (Fig 94) — Points to Remember

1. It is very important that the move before the ball-out is performed well if a successful ball-out is to be achieved. It is assumed here that the preceding move is a crash dive, and that the ball-out is a barani. If the crash dive is short of rotation, the performer will have to duck under too early — this will result in the legs being too far over the face when the performer lands in the back drop position. The ball-out barani will then be short of rotation and the form will suffer. Alternatively, if the crash dive is over-rotated, the performer will land in the back drop position but on his or her bottom, with the head, shoulders and back off the bed. It will then be very difficult for the performer to hold the legs still — unless he or she has very strong abdominal muscles. As a result, the ball-out will end up very low and again the form will suffer.

2. The old school of trampoline coaching used to teach the back drop landing so that the performer's head was off the bed. However, when it was realised that the hip extension and knee kick caused the shoulders and head to press into the bed (as a result of action/reaction) it became obvious to coaches that the head and shoulders should be on the bed. Performers should be careful as once they have learned to keep their head off the bed, the habit is very hard to break.

3. A very skilled trampolinist can move the ball-out forwards, backwards or keep it on the spot. This is achieved by changing the direction of hip extension in relation to the bed. Consequently, if a performer lands from the crash dive close to the springs, he or she would have to extend the hips either backwards or forwards into the ball-out (depending on which end of the trampoline is closest) in order to centralise the ball-out.

4. As the performer lands in the back drop, the knees must be locked and the stomach muscles held firm as the bed is being depressed. The performer must also

hold the arms firm so that all body movement occurs at the bottom of the bed. The body-weight will cause the bed to depress by a certain amount, but hip extension and knee kick will depress it further.

Cody (Figs 95 – 100)

The cody is the name given to a backwards somersault from the front drop position. The cody is always learned from a lazy back because the transfer of backward momentum is carried on to the cody from the lazy back. It would be a waste of time for performers to try to learn the cody from a front drop because they would be trying to somersault backwards after having initiated forward rotation through carrying out the front drop.

After executing a normal lazy back (three-quarter back somersault to front drop) and landing with the arms and legs in the correct position (arms bent at the elbows, with the elbows out to the sides and the knees bent at a ninety degree angle), the performer then flicks the legs straight and pushes hard on the trampoline with the arms and hands as the trampoline bed recoils. Once the backward rotation has been initiated and the performer has left the bed, the required position can be taken up. Figs 96 and 97 show the landing of the lazy back and the knee kick into the cody — when the tucked position is taken up the cody resembles the back somersault tucked with the straight line-out at the end. The performer should learn the correctly timed knee kick by performing a lazy back carry through to a back drop in the straight position; until the timing of the knee kick is

Figs 95 – 100   Cody.

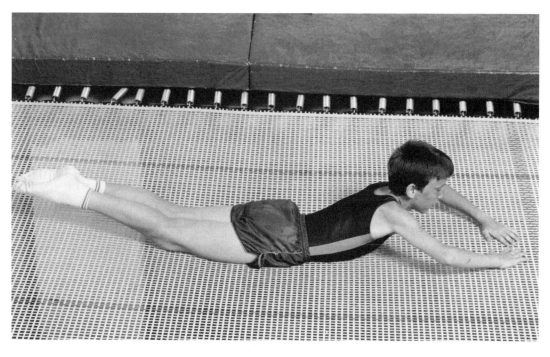

Fig 96

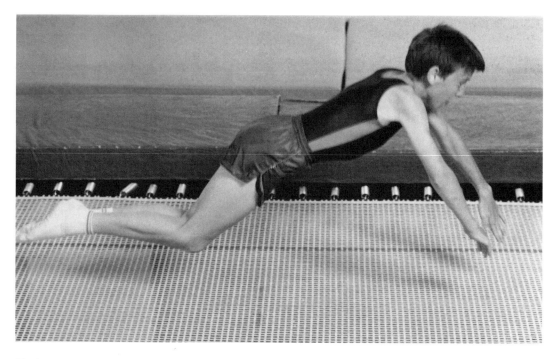

Fig 97

Fig 98

correct every time and until plenty of rotation is produced, the cody should not be attempted.

Obviously safety precautions must be taken, such as the use of a spotting rig, the use of crash mat and/or with the coach spotting. One of the safest ways to learn a cody is to have the crash mat pushed in by fellow performers whilst the coach stands in to support, assisting with hip lift or catching the performer should he or she mistime the knee kick. A slight 'kip' would give the performer extra height which would make it easier for the coach to support him or her. The coach must be very careful not to 'kill' the performer's bounce as the performer takes off for the cody. For a description of kipping and killing, *see* pages 79 and 80.

Fig 99

Fig 100

Mechanics of the Cody
(Fig 101) — (Points to Remember)

1. The back cody is discussed here as the front cody is rarely used in competition. The lazy back is generally the move performed before the cody in a routine although many others can be used. If the lazy back is performed before the cody, it is best if it is over-rotated rather than under-rotated as the lower body will land slightly before the trunk and the 'kaboom' action that results (*see* Glossary) will push the trunk further into the bed — thus helping the trampolinist rotate for the cody. If the lazy back is under rotated however, the upper body will land before the knees, thighs and hips and the kaboom action will work against the performer.

2. As the performer lands from the lazy back, the knees should be bent so that the lower legs are just short of vertical. By kicking the legs from the knee joints, an action/reaction results so that the chest is pushed into the trampoline bed and rotation is aided. Apart from this kicking movement, the weight of the lower legs themselves produce still more transfer of momentum and thus rotation as they are blocked.

3. The timing of the hands being thrust on the trampoline bed should coincide with the blocking of the knee kick. Performers must be careful not to assume the rotating shape too quickly and should allow the shoulders to start moving first.

4. Some coaches prefer the first part of the cody phased; for example the performer can show a quarter of a somersault (in a straight position) before tucking or piking. *The Trampoline Handbook* indicates that if the performer manages a twelve o'clock kick-out, no points will be deducted by the

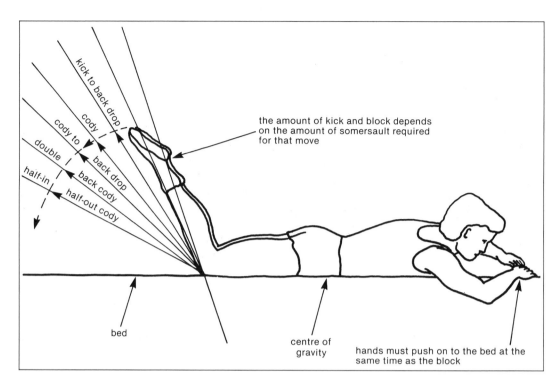

the amount of kick and block depends on the amount of somersault required for that move

kick to back drop

cody

cody to back drop

double

back cody

half-in

half-out cody

bed

centre of gravity

hands must push on to the bed at the same time as the block

Fig 101   Mechanics of the cody.

judges. However, I prefer the performer to go for an early kick-out and ignore the phased beginning.

One-and-three-quarter Front Somersault (Figs 102—9)

When performed by the experienced trampolinist the one-and-three-quarter front somersault should resemble a front somersault for the first half of the move and a crash dive for the latter half of the move. It must be stressed that nothing looks worse than an early line-out which is immediately broken due to either insufficient height or rotation. If the performer has a shortage of height or rotation it would be much better for him or her to line out later, holding that line-out throughout the remainder of the move. As more height and hip lift are created through practice, the line-out can

Figs 102–109   A one-and-three-quarter front somersault piked. Plenty of hip lift is needed so that the performer can line out at the end of the move.

always be brought in earlier. However, when learning a one-and-three-quarter front somersault the last thing a performer thinks about is the line-out. The end of the move should be learned in the same way as the crash dive was learned (with the performer gradually straightening out at the end as he or she gains more confidence). The beginning of the move consists of the same take-off as for the front somersault, but with more hip lift and with the arms being thrown up and over more vigorously. Throwing the arms downwards causes both a loss of height and control. The crash mat should be used to increase the performer's confidence and to kill the recoil of the trampoline bed — the performer will not have the added worry of working out of the new move. Many performers like their coach to call 'out' at the moment when they

Fig 103

Fig 104

Fig 105

Fig 106

should be preparing to open for the landing. The coach should call this slightly early so that by the time the performer has heard the call and reacted, it will not be too late.

The one-and-three-quarter somersault should be initially learned in the tucked position. For the first few attempts the performer will probably come out of the tucked position with just enough time to land in a back drop position. As soon as the coach calls, the performer should look for the trampoline bed below so that a well-timed opening can be judged with sufficient time available for fine landing adjustments. Looking for the bed, or 'spotting' the bed, is an important concept when progressing on to double somersaults.

Once the one-and-three-quarter front somersault tucked has been mastered a piked one-and-three-quarter front somersault can be learned. It has exactly the

Fig 107

same take-off as in the tucked position but has slightly more hip lift. With the one-and-three-quarter piked it is actually easier to spot the bed than in the tucked position because the performer rotates more slowly and the pike is a more open position.

KIPPING AND KILLING THE BOUNCE

'Kipping' is the technique used to produce additional height to the performer's bounce. Standing level with the trampoline, the coach uses his or her weight to depress the bed just before the performer makes contact with the bed. The coach then removes his or her weight from the trampoline at the exact moment when the performer has fully depressed the bed — this results in a recoil power equal to the weight of both performer and coach being

Fig 108

Fig 109

applied to the performer alone. This technique can be very helpful to the performer when learning a new move, however, because the height has been created with the help of someone other than the performer alone, it may be extremely difficult for him or her to control. This technique should therefore not be played around with unnecessarily and should be left to the experts to be used as an aid to performance, not as a game.

'Killing' the bed is achieved by the coach adding his or her weight to the trampoline a fraction of a second after the performer lands and remaining in contact with the bed in order to absorb the recoil power of the trampoline. It should be noted that the difference between kipping and killing the bed is a matter of very precise timing and so should be left to the very experienced coach.

COMPETITIONS

Before moving on to describing double somersaults, competitions and routine building are discussed. When performers reach the stage at which they are learning multiple somersaults they are becoming quite advanced and therefore will probably have already entered many competitions.

There are many trampolining competitions held all over the country. Each region holds a closed championship which allows only competitors from that area to enter. Every area also holds an open championship and in this case competitors from all over the country are invited to compete. For example, the South West Open Championships are held in, and organised by, the South West Trampoline Division and are open to competitors from any division. The South West Closed Championships however, are again held and put on by the South West Trampoline Division but are open only to competitors living in the region. Open championships tend to begin at a rather advanced level and so a closed championship would be more suitable as a first competition. Some divisions hold quite a few novice events which are also ideal for performers entering their first competition — they are not open to performers who have competed on the open circuit (as open championships are called) and are not open to competitors who have won previously at the novice level.

Every competition has a compulsory (or set) routine. This is decided by the division when holding novice and closed competitions, however for open competitions the National Set Routines are used. These National Set Routines are standard and are used all over the world for national, international and world championships. Every competitor has to perform the set routine first and every routine consists of ten different moves with each age group having a different set routine. There used to be an under-11 age group for competitions but it has been discontinued, although divisions are trying to bring it back. At present the national set routines are as follows:

Under-13 Age Group

1. Straight back
2. Straddle jump
3. Tuck back to seat
4. Half twist to feet
5. Half-twist jump
6. Tuck jump
7. Pike back
8. Piked barani
9. Pike jump
10. Pike front

Under-15 Age Group

1. Straight lazy back
2. Cody (tucked)
3. Straddle jump
4. Straight back somersault
5. Straight barani
6. One-and-a-quarter back somersault tucked to back drop
7. Half twist to feet
8. Back somersault tucked
9. Crash dive
10. Tucked barani ball-out

In the under-18 age group and the mens' and ladies' open competitions there are only five compulsory moves with the competitors adding another five of their own choice. The moves can be done in any order, and the difficulty factor is not taken into consideration for the competitor's own choice of moves. The five compulsory moves for the under-18 age group and open mens' and ladies' are as follows:

Under-18 Age Group

1. Full
2. Piked barani
3. Free barani ball-out
4. Free one-and-three-quarter front somersault
5. Straight back

Mens' and Ladies' Open

1. Half-in half-out tucked
2. Double full
3. Free one-and-three-quarter front somersault
4. Straight barani
5. Rudi ball-out

Note: 'free' means the move can be

performed in a position of the competitor's choice.

Any competitor of any age who is able to complete a routine consisting of the five set moves can enter the mens' and ladies' open competitions.

Judging

Each judge in a competition notes down deductions for faults and marks the routine out of ten, provided the required ten moves are completed. Judges look for good height throughout the routine and check to see that the performer does not travel too far (staying within a square metre of the centre of the trampoline is considered perfect). Competitors should show good stretching of the knees and feet and a good body alignment throughout each movement. They should also line out, hold each line-out until landing and stay in control until the end of the routine. A perfect movement in a routine will have no points deducted; a very good move which is just slightly lacking in height or stretch or which may contain a slight bit of travel would get a deduction of 0.1 points; an average move which has room for improvement would have a 0.2 point deduction; a poor move would have a 0.3 point deduction; a very bad move with many faults would have a 0.4 point deduction; and a move that contains every fault possible and only just resembles the move it is meant to represent will get a 0.5 point deduction. Fig 110 gives the possible deductions for an above average routine and the following shows how the final score is calculated:

Move number	Deduction
1	0.2
2	0.1
3	0.2
4	0.2
5	0.3
6	0.2
7	0.1
8	0.1
9	0.2
10	0.3
Total deductions 1.9	

Fig 110   Possible deductions for an above average routine.

Take the total deductions (1.9) away from the total the routine is marked out of (which in this case is 10.0) to calculate the judge's score: $10.0 - 1.9 = 8.1$.

Tariffing

Every competitor has to perform the set routine in the first round; in the second round every performer has to complete a routine of ten different moves, of his or her own choice. This second routine is called the voluntary routine and is judged in the same way as the set routine, but the degree of difficulty of each move is taken into consideration in the voluntary scores. The degree of difficulty of a performer's routine is the 'tariff'.

Every individual move has its own tariff which is worked out in the following way: for every quarter somersault 0.1 points are awarded; for every half twist 0.1 points are awarded; if a move is performed where at least one whole somersault is completed in either the piked or straight position an extra 0.1 points are given. The following list gives the tariffs of various individual moves:

All shaped jumps   no tariff
Seat drop   no tariff
Back drop (one-quarter somersault)   0.1
Front drop (one-quarter somersault)   0.1
Half twist to feet from seat drop   0.1
Half twist to feet from back/front drop   0.2
Back pullover (three-quarter somersault)   0.3
Lazy back (three-quarter somersault)   0.3
Crash dive (three-quarter somersault)   0.3
Front somersault tucked   0.4
Back somersault tucked   0.4
Piked/straight back   0.5
Front somersault piked   0.5
Barani (any shape)   0.5
Tucked cody (one-and-a-quarter somersault)   0.5
Piked cody   0.6
Ball-out barani (One-and-a-quarter somersault with a half twist)   0.6
Full twisting back somersault (one somersault (0.4) plus one twist (0.2)   0.6
Rudi (one somersault (0.4) plus one-and-a-half twist (0.3))   0.7
Double full (one somersault (0.4) plus two twists (0.4))   0.8
One-and-three-quarter front somersault tucked   0.7
One-and-three-quarter front somersault piked   0.8

In a competition every performer must hand in a completed tariff sheet, this shows the routine the performer aims to complete – an example of one before it has been filled in is shown in Fig 111.

Name:		Age group:	
Club:		Competitor's no:	
Move	Tariff		Tariff check
1.			
2.			
3.			
4.			
5.			
6.			
7.			
8.			
9.			
10.			
Total			

Fig 111   The layout of a tariff sheet before it has been filled in.

Every age group in a competition has a tariff judge. This job is not an easy one as the tariff judge has to check each performer's routine; if it differs from the sheet the different moves have to be jotted down and tariffed. It does not matter if the performer does a different routine from that on their tariff sheet as long as ten different moves are performed. If the performer completes ten moves but one or more is repeated, each repeated move loses its tariff value. For example, the following routine would be tariffed as shown:

1. Straight back somersault   0.5
2. Full twisting back somersault   0.6
3. Straight barani   0.5

4.	Back somersault piked	0.5
5.	Rudi	0.5
6.	Straight back somersault (repeated tariff: points deducted)	(0.5)
7.	Straight barani (repeated tariff: points deducted)	(0.5)
8.	Back somersault tucked	0.4
9.	Crash dive	0.3
10.	Barani ball-out	0.6

Total tariff   3.9

If performers complete less than ten moves, then they are marked out of the number of moves that are done and are tariffed for all of those moves. If more than ten moves are performed, the routine stops being tariffed and judged at the tenth move and a whole mark (1.0) is taken away for every extra move that is performed.

In the under-18 age group and the open mens' or ladies' groups a tariff sheet must also be handed in for the set routine. Although the tariff is not taken into account in the set routine, the routine must be completed exactly as it is written on the sheet. If the performer's set routine differs from his or her announced routine it is terminated at the first incorrect move — if the first five moves were correct and the sixth move was incorrect, the routine would only be marked out of five. When writing out tariff sheets for set routines, the five set moves in the routine must have an asterisk by them.

An example of a sensible under-18 set routine would be:

1. Straight back somersault*
2. Rudi
3. Back somersault piked
4. Barani
5. Straddle jump

6.	Tucked back somersault
7.	Piked barani*
8.	Full*
9.	One-and-three-quarter front somersault tucked*
10.	Rudi ball-out*

The asterisk (*) indicates the five set moves of the routine.

Scoring

The panel consists of five form judges, a superior judge and a tariff judge. The five form judges each give a score for the set performance. The highest and lowest scores are disregarded and the remaining three are added together. The superior judge checks the marks to see that the discrepancy between the three middle marks is no more than 0.1 for marks of 9.0 and above; 0.2 for marks of 8.5 up to, but not including 9.0; and 0.3 for marks below 8.5. If these three marks do not conform with the above rules then the middle mark from the three is trebled. In the voluntary routine the same system applies, with the tariff being added to the three middle marks. The set scores for each performer are then added to their voluntary scores:

Set routine scores: 8.1, (8.3), 8.1, 8.2, (8.0). Total = 24.4.
First voluntary routine scores: 7.2, 7.1, 7.1, (6.9), (7.5). Total = 21.4 plus a 5.2 tariff. Total score of first voluntary routine = 26.6. The set total score of 24.4 plus the first voluntary total score of 26.6 = the overall total of 51.0.

If a set of marks was as follows: 8.1, 7.8, 7.9, 8.9, 8.9, then the scores 7.8 and 8.9 (the highest and lowest scores) would be knocked off. However, this would leave too large a discrepancy between 7.9 and 8.9 — 8.1 being the middle mark, would therefore be trebled.

Once everyone competing in a particular group has finished the first two rounds, the top ten scores compete in the finals. The competitors perform in reverse order in the finals — the person who was lying in tenth position competes first, finishing with the performer who was leading the competition. The final scores are then added to scores from the first two rounds to give a grand total for each performer. The finalists can either perform the same voluntary routine during the second round, or, according to their score they can compete tactically using a higher or lower tariff. If the leader has a good margin the tariff for the final could be reduced, hopefully improving the form.

Superior judges organise the competition: they ensure that the five judges are watching the performer who is about to compete and that all competitors have a warm-up; they check on spotters and the tariff judge and call out all the marks for the recorder. The recorder writes down all the scores for each performer during each round, adds the totals of each round and so works out who the finalists are and writes their names down in reverse order. As the finalists compete, the recorder does the same again and at the end of the competition every performer in the age group is given a placing.

The officials do not have a very easy job, and as there are four age groups — under-13, under-15, under-18 and mens' and ladies' opens, eight compeitions are run throughout the day. As there are hundreds of competitors at these trampoline competitions, many officials are needed. Performers must therefore be prepared for a long, tiring day when

Fig 112   *Alison Stuart competing in the South West Closed Championships.*

entering their first open or closed competition.

Competition Clothing

In open, national and international championships, the clothing rules are very strict: no jewellery 'whatsoever' must be worn; girls must wear white footwear below the ankles and leotards with long sleeves; boys must wear long whites (which usually have braces) with a leotard vest underneath and white footwear; footwear can be socks or trampoline shoes — a non-slip sole being preferable.

Lower level competitions usually have more lenient rules on clothing — boys may wear shorts and T-shirts and girls may wear short-sleeved leotards or swim-suits.

Team Competitions

In trampolining competitions teams can also be entered. In national competitions the teams are usually made up of three or four club members competing against clubs from all over the country whereas in international competitions the teams can be members from different clubs. Three or four competitors make up a team. If four competitors are entered, then the best three set and first voluntary scores count, however, all four team members receive a medal if the team wins.

National Championships

The British National Championships in trampolining are held every year. There is a championship for every age group as well as open mens' and ladies' championships to find the overall British champions at every level.

To qualify for the British National Championships a performer must have scored 22.5 in a set routine (an average score of 7.5) and also have reached the finals in one open competition during the year. The British National Championship placings are looked at very carefully by national coaches in order to pick performers for regional zone training squads and then national squads. It is performers from these squads that are picked to represent the UK at international level.

Synchro

Synchronised trampolining consists of two performers competing side by side as a team. Two trampolines are placed next to each other (two metres apart) with a performer on each trampoline. Both performers start bouncing together and start the routine at the same time; the idea being to keep a mirror image. Synchro marks are judged in the same way as form marks — by deductions. As the performers land from each move a deduction of between 0 and 0.5 points is given. If they land in perfect timing a 0 point deduction is given; likewise if the performers are so out of synchronisation that they are almost bouncing alternately, a 0.5 point deduction is given. The deductions are added together and taken away from 10.0 to give a final synchro score. If the performers are so out of synchronisation that they are on different moves, then both routines are terminated and marked out of however many moves were performed in reasonable synchronisation. The same happens if the competitors perform a different move half-way through the routine.

There are two synchro judges and the two resulting synchro marks are averaged and then doubled. There are also three form judges for each person and the middle two marks they provide are added together with the synchro marks to give the score for each round. A tariff is added if the round is a voluntary one.

Synchronised trampolining competitions are only really held at the national level, however every international competition (such as the World and European Championships) has a synchro event for both men and women. There are also many international competitions held all over the world solely for synchro performance.

7 Multiple Somersaults and their Advanced Work-ups

Half-out Fliffis

This consists of a double front somersault with a half twist in the second somersault. The take-off for the half-out fliffis is just like that for a fast, high one-and-three-quarter front somersault and the ending feels like a barani ball-out — here are two perfect work-ups.

The performer can start by practising a double front somersault to the feet with the crash mat pushed in, or alternatively, a one-and-three-quarter front somersault with plenty of hip lift and an early straight kick to land in a flat back drop on the crash mat is just as good. The next step in learning this move is, after the performer has practised many fast, high, one-and-three-quarter front somersaults on the crash mat, to incorporate the half twist. The trampolinist should perform the twist as the opening of the one-and-three-quarter work-up begins. If performers attempt to learn the move by doing double front somersault work-ups then it will probably take longer to learn the half-out as they try to edge their way around the twist bit by bit. Also in attempting the double front somersault, performers lose sight of the bed and hence tend to twist too late. With the one-and-three-quarter front work-up however, the bed is kept in sight throughout the twist — this is the correct technique.

After the performer has got over the initial anticipation of the first few half-outs more hip lift can be incorporated and the performer can concentrate on spotting the bed before beginning the twist. When the trampolinist is competent at performing this move, the half-out should be lined out of, with the arms kept by the side during the twist. When learning to do this move in a piked position (as shown in Figs 114 – 19), the work-up simply consists of a fast, high, one-and-three-quarter front piked with plenty of hip lift and an early opening onto the crash mat. Then, as with the tucked half-out, the twist is performed as the opening occurs with the trampoline mat in sight throughout the twist.

The tariff for the tucked half-out is 0.9 and for the piked half-out, 1.0 (eight-quarters of a somersault making 0.8 points, one half of a twist making 0.1 points with an extra 0.1 points when the move is performed in the piked position).

Double Back Somersault

The double back is not a particularly difficult move to learn; it simply takes commitment. However, commitment to some performers is not that simple and to build up their confidence they need plenty of work-ups. The best work-up for the double back is for performers to practise a very fast one-and-a-quarter back somersault to back drop from a single small bounce. The

Fig 113   Erika Phelps performing a lazy back.

reason the move should be performed low on the trampoline is so that the performer can get used to producing the required rotation that is needed for the double back.

When the performer feels ready to have a go at the move the crash mat should be pushed in and the coach should stand in at the end of the move to assist on landing (if an overhead rig is not available). If the

performer is lacking rotation the coach may need to assist by pushing on the lower back as the performer comes round for the second somersault. However, this is rarely a problem for performers in the very beginning, in fact they usually pull back too much with the head and shoulders. This pull back is called 'snatching' the move because the initial 'pick-up' rotation is rushed and the move commences before

Fig 114 – 19   The half-out piked showing
plenty of hip lift and a straight line-out
throughout the twist.

Fig 115

Fig 116

Fig 117

Fig 118

full height and leg extension has been
achieved on the take-off. The snatching
leaves the performer insufficient height and
control and as it is difficult for the bed to be
spotted, the landing will not be stable.

The performer should be encouraged to
swing the arms very vigorously up past the
waist and to block them at shoulder level.
The legs should be extending and the hips
pushed forwards a little as the arms are
blocking. This technique will give a high,
controlled, double back somersault making
it easier for the performer to spot the bed at
the finish and to line out with the arms by
the sides before they are lifted up in preparation for the following move.

The piked double back is simply a matter
of producing more rotation. Whether performing the move in a piked or tucked
position, it is important for the performer
not to pull the arms back out of line with the
head — this leads to an open piked or
tucked position with the head back out of
line throughout the somersault and is
untidy. If the head is in line on take-off then
it will always be easier for the performer to
pull the required position into a tidy shape

Fig 119

with the head following the line of the tuck or pike.

The double back tucked has a tariff of 0.8 with the piked position receiving an extra 0.1 points to make it a tariff 0.9.

Half-in Half-out Fliffis

This move consists of a half twist followed by a half-out fliffis. The last part of the move (the half-out) has already been learned, so it is the beginning of the move that the performer needs to practise.

The first thing the performer needs to do is to ensure that he or she can successfully complete a square half twist to front drop. The difficult part of the manoeuvre is trying to duck under (making the move a half twist to crash dive) but still keeping it square. Most performers cannot keep the shape square when first learning the half twist to crash dive. The arms must be swung close together up to the blocking position. As the arms block, the hips are lifted forwards and upwards and one shoulder is pulled back a fraction. However, the shoulder must not be pulled back before blocking (this is called 'going round the corner') or the somersault will rotate diagonally.

When the half twist to crash dive is mastered, the performer can attempt to pick up slightly more rotation which is required for a half twist to front somersault. Each time performers attempt to gain more rotation, they may be tempted to go round the corner — this must be avoided. The next work-up is the half twist to one-and-three-quarter front somersault. When this is mastered with plenty of rotation being produced and an early opening to a flat back drop the performer is in the same learning position as when doing a half-out. However, it must be remembered that if a performer learns the half-in half-out too

quickly and repeatedly performs the move with bad technique, learning will be hindered in the future.

The tariff of a half-in half-out in a tucked position is 1.0 and in a piked position, 1.1.

Rudi-out Fliffis

This consists of a double front somersault with one-and-a-half twist in the second somersault. The best work-up for the rudi-out is the rudi ball-out. In the rudi ball-out the performer comes off the bed with the knee kick, spots the bed and then wraps the arms in for the rudi. The movements are the same in the rudi-out, except the performer does a one-and-a-quarter somersault before spotting the bed. The performer usually learns the move in a tucked position before progressing to performing it in a piked position. This means that the feeling of opening from the tuck, wrapping in for the twist by kicking for a ball-out and then taking up a shallow tucked shape quickly before twisting can be simulated. The tuck must not be held for long otherwise the performer will lose sight of the bed.

When performing a rudi-out the twist must be started a little earlier than in the half-out, so that it is completed with plenty of time left to prepare for the landing. When first learning the rudi-out performers often twist a little too late, finishing the twist with no room for adjustment at the end. Performers may even start the twist in the correct place but complete it with insufficient time to make adjustments at the end. Either the performer is too low or the twist is too slow. If the twist is too slow, the performer should ensure that the arms are kept close in to the body during the twist and that the body is very straight with the head in line with it. Bad body alignment slows down the twist. The tariff of a rudi-out tucked is 1.1 and in a piked position it is 1.2.

Other twisting double somersaults, such as the barani-in back-out (a double front somersault with a half twist in the first somersault), the full-in back-out (a double back somersault with a full twist in the first somersault) or a rudi-in back-out (a double front somersault with one-and-a-half twists in the first somersault) can be worked up to in exactly the same way as the double back was. For example, when learning a rudi-in back-out, the performer would initially practise a low rudi to back drop to experience the rotation that is needed to perform a high rudi-in back-out. However, these three moves are very rarely, if ever, used by performers because it is much more difficult to create sufficient rotation when twisting in the first somersault, compared with twisting in the second somersault.

Full-in Half-out (Pucked)

This is a forward double somersault with one-and-a-half twists, the twist lasting throughout the somersaults. When the move is broken down, it resembles a barani in the first three-quarters of the somersault, another half twist during the next half somersault, followed by a barani-out. The move is usually learned in the 'pucked' position – this is only used when twisting in multiple somersaults and is similar to a shallow tucked position with the arms folded across the chest. This looks very messy however, if the legs are not held closely together. The full-in half-out can also be performed in a semi-piked position and is then called a full-in half-out (straight legs). The tariffs are the same for both positions (1.1) because a complete somersault without a twist is not performed.

The first work-up for this move should be a barani to back drop and the second a barani to back with another half twist just before the landing thus making the landing position a front drop. When landing in the front drop performers must be careful not to throw themselves down. The take-off should be an 'up and over'. The move can then be ducked under ending in a flat back drop. When plenty of rotation has been created and the work-up is square (down the middle of the trampoline) on take-off, the trampolinist can complete the move by performing the barani-out at the end. Each work-up must be perfected before moving on to the next stage and a crash mat should be used for all stages. The take-off must be a 'turn before twist' – if the performer were to twist off the mat then he or she would be severely lacking in rotation and not very square on landing. The twist must not be rushed and the one-and-a-half twist should last throughout the whole of the double somersault.

Back-in Full-out

This move consists of a double back somersault with a full twist in the second somersault. It is performed as a tucked back somersault for the first half of the move. The performer then opens out into the pucked postion, completes a half twist in order to spot the bed and then finishes off with the remaining half twist – the eyes are on the trampoline bed throughout this twist.

To work up to this move the trampolinist initially performs a tucked back somersault with a late half twist on coming out of the tucked position. When performing the completed back-in full-out, twisting should not be initiated in the first somersault, however, for this first work-up stage it is necessary to twist at the end of the first somersault. In the second work-up stage the performer progresses to a front drop landing and in this case the twist can be carried out between the end of the first somersault and the front drop landing. It is during the next work-up that the performer can really begin to take time over the twist. This work-up requires the performer to duck under the back-in half twist to front drop. During this work-up the twist should not be initiated during the first somersault. If a performer were to initiate the twist in the back-in full-out too early during a competition, the superior judge could say the move was a half-in half-out — if a half-in half-out had already been performed in the voluntary section then the competitor would lose a 1.0 tariff for repeating the move. Performers must therefore ensure that when learning the move, the correct placing of the twist is mastered in the back-in half twist to duck under work-up.

The performer should spot the bed on opening out of the tuck and again after the first half twist has been completed. When the performer feels ready to attempt the whole move, the bed can be spotted throughout the final part of the move until landing. As long as the back-in full-out is blocked on take-off with the head kept in line, the performer should be able to complete the move with a neat tight tuck in the first somersault and a tidy, tight pucked position throughout the twist in the second somersault. This move is not as difficult to learn as many other twisting double somersaults because the performer cannot twist off the mat. The back-in full-out has a tariff of 1.0.

Full-in Full-out

This move consists of a double back somersault with a twist in each somersault and is learned in the same way as the back-in full-out, except that the performer starts with a full twisting back somersault.

The first work-up the performer must master is a pucked full twisting back somersault. This must be initiated with the arms kept close to the body as they swing past the hips ('narrow' arms) so that the performer does not overtwist. It is during the next work-up that the performer has a little wider arms on take-off as this work-up incorporates an extra half twist. As soon as the performer can, he or she should practise a pucked one-and-a-half twisting back somersault to a front drop landing. This extra amount of somersault enables the performer to slow down the twist. The one-and-a-half twist must last for the whole one-and-a-quarter somersault in this work-up. In the next work-up, the twist can be slowed down once again with the performer ducking under. The bed must be spotted as the performer comes round in the third half twist. It is then just a matter of time and confidence before the performer can complete the last half twist towards the end of the move, keeping the eyes on the trampoline bed throughout the move.

The full-in full-out should have a half twist in each half of each somersault with the legs extended and the arms and body lined out at the end of the move. It is very important to initiate this move with narrow arms (kept close to the body) and square hips before one shoulder is pulled back to initiate the twist, If the move is not square when initiated then it is very difficult to keep the puck neat with the legs together, and both the height and rotation would be inadequate if the twist was 'snatched' off the bed on take-off. As with the full-in half-out, this move can be carried out with straight legs. The tariff of the full-in full-out is 1.2.

8 Routine Building

It is very important for a performer to learn how to build a ten-bounce routine incorporating as many sensible link-ups as possible. For example, it is wise for a performer to avoid doing any of the following:

1. Linking more than two forward movements together — this tends to result in a loss of height.

Fig 120 Erika Phelps perfoming a pike back drop.

2. Performing codys, ball-outs or pull-overs in the middle of a routine. These are best at the end of the routine, or if essential, at the beginning when the perfomer has enough moves left in the routine to build up the height again. In the middle of a routine these moves (especially a ball-out) cause tremendous loss in height and the routine would be over before the performer had a chance to rebuild the height. In fact, it is best to leave any non-feet landing position to the end of the routine, whether it be a cody, ball-out, pullover or a seat drop or back drop with a half twist to the feet.
3. Linking more than two or three backward moves since, although the height is maintained, the performer will eventually run out of room.

So ideally, it is best to link together moves as follows: forward, backward, forward, backward and so on; with the perfomer staying on the feet as much as possible. This will make it much easier for the performer to keep the moves high and close to the middle of the bed.

The following gives an idea of how an individual may build up routines from a beginner's level to an advanced level as he or she progresses.

Routine 1

1.	Pike back	0.5
2.	Straddle jump	0.0
3.	Tuck back	0.4
4.	Seat drop	0.0
5.	Half twist to seat drop	0.1

6.	Half twist to feet	0.1
7.	Tuck jump	0.0
8.	Half-twist jump	0.1
9.	Pike jump	0.0
10.	Pike front	0.5
	Total tariff	1.7

The above routine would be suitable for a performer at novice level. Obviously there would be no point in using this routine, or the next one in the open circuit because they are not as difficult as the set routine — unless the under-11 age group was brought back to open competitions.

Routine 2

1.	Straight back somersault	0.5
2.	Straddle jump	0.0
3.	Pike back	0.5
4.	Straddle jump	0.0
5.	Tuck back	0.4
6.	Seat drop	0.0
7.	Half twist to seat drop	0.1
8.	Half twist to feet	0.1
9.	Pike jump	0.0
10.	Front somersault piked	0.5
	Total tariff	2.1

A straddle jump is included twice in Routine 2, although it was mentioned earlier that moves should not be repeated. Although a performer will lose the tariff if a move is duplicated, the straddle jump has no tariff and it is of no loss to repeat the move. As it is the most stable jump to perform between somersaults it is sensible to use it to its full benefit.

Routine 3

1.	Straight back somersault	0.5
2.	Straddle jump	0.0
3.	Piked back somersault	0.5

4.	Straddle jump	0.0
5.	Tucked back somersault	0.4
6.	Tucked back somersault to seat	0.4
7.	Half twist to feet	0.1
8.	Half-twist jump	0.1
9.	Pike jump	0.0
10.	Piked front somersault	0.5
	Total tariff	2.5

As the routines incorporate a greater variety of somersaults, the smaller moves such as the seat drop half twist to seat drop (which cause dramatic height loss) are becoming more infrequent.

Routine 4

1.	Straight back somersault	0.5
2.	Straight barani	0.5
3.	Straddle jump	0.0
4.	Pike back	0.5
5.	Straddle jump	0.0
6.	Tuck back	0.4
7.	Tuck back to seat	0.4
8.	Half twist to feet	0.1
9.	Pike jump	0.0
10.	Piked front somersault	0.5
	Total tariff	2.9

Routine 5

1.	Straight back somersault	0.5
2.	Straight barani	0.5
3.	Pike back	0.5
4.	Tucked barani	0.5
5.	Tuck back	0.4
6.	Tuck back to seat	0.4
7.	Half twist to feet	0.1
8.	Half twist jump	0.1
9.	Pike jump	0.0
10.	Pike front/Pike barani	0.5/0.6
	Total tariff	3.5/3.6

Routine Building

As the performer becomes more advanced and more somersaults are learned, the jumps can be taken out thus pushing up the total tariffs. It is important to remember that the form score (as given by the judges) is tripled whereas the tariff is only added to the total score once. This means that the performer will not benefit by pushing the tariff up if form scores are sacrificed. Performers should practise higher tariff moves in training but should make sure that in competitions the routine used is well within their capabilities. This is safer and means there is less chance of the performer failing and so he or she will gain good form marks.

Routine 6

1.	Straight back somersault	0.5
2.	Straight barani	0.5
3.	Back somerault piked	0.5
4.	Tucked barani	0.5
5.	Back somersault tucked to seat	0.4
6.	Half twist to feet	0.1
7.	Back somersault tucked	0.4
8.	Crash dive	0.3
9.	Barani ball-out	0.6
10.	Front somersault piked	0.5
	Total tariff	4.3

Routine 7

1.	Straight back	0.5
2.	Full twisting back	0.6
3.	Barani	0.5
4.	Back somersault piked	0.5
5.	Tucked barani	0.5
6.	Tuck back to seat	0.4
7.	Half twist to feet	0.1
8.	Tuck back	0.4
9.	Crash dive	0.3
10.	Barani ball-out	0.6
	Total tariff	4.4

The next routine can be the same as Routine 7 but with the crash dive being replaced with a one-and-three-quarter front somersault tucked (with a tariff of 0.7), making the total tariff 4.8. A one-and-three-quarter front somersault piked can then be used in the routine, giving a total tariff of 4.9. The next move to be added to the routine is usually a half-out or a rudi, which means that the tuck back to seat can be taken out at last!

Routine 8

1.	Half-out tucked	0.9
2.	Straight back	0.5
3.	Barani	0.5
4.	Tuck back	0.4
5.	Full twisting back	0.6
6.	Tucked barani	0.5
7.	Pike back	0.5
8.	One-and-three-quarter front somersault piked	0.8
9.	Barani ball-out	0.6
10.	Front somersault piked	0.5
	Total tariff	5.8

When a large jump in the tariff occurs — as seen in Routine 7's 4.9 to Routine 8's 5.8 — form is usually sacrificed. It is therefore probably best for a performer to keep a 4.9 tariff routine in competition until he or she can reliably complete the 5.8 tariff routine. It must also be remembered that it probably takes a performer at least five years to progress through the routines covered so far (from the 1.7 tariff to the 5.8 tariff), depending on how often he or she trains.

When the performer has mastered the 5.8 tariff routine, he or she can then try a routine starting with a half-out piked; the next sensible progression would probably be a rudi.

Routine 9

1.	Half-out fliffis piked	1.0
2.	Straight back	0.5
3.	Straight barani	0.5
4.	Pike back	0.5
5.	Rudi	0.7
6.	Tuck back	0.4
7.	Full	0.6
8.	Tucked barani	0.5
9.	One-and-three-quarter front somersault piked	0.8
10.	Barani ball-out	0.6
	Total tariff	6.1

The next progression is usually to put two half-outs into the routine, separated by a straight back or any other back somersault.

Routine 10

1.	Half-out piked	1.0
2.	Straight back	0.5
3.	Half-out tucked	0.9
4.	Barani	0.5
5.	Tuck back	0.4
6.	Rudi	0.7
7.	Pike back	0.5
8.	Full	0.6
9.	One-and-three-quarter front somersault piked	0.8
10.	Barani ball-out	0.6
	Total tariff	6.5

The next progressions depend upon whether the performer is more capable at somersaulting or twisting. The next move to be incorporated into the routine could be a rudi ball-out, a double twisting back somersault (double full) or a double back. Presuming that the performer prefers to somersault rather than twist (which is usually the case) the next progression would look something like Routine 11.

Routine 11

1.	Half-out piked	1.0
2.	Straight back	0.5
3.	Half-out tucked	0.9
4.	Double back somersault tucked	0.8
5.	Barani	0.5
6.	Full	0.6
7.	Rudi	0.7
8.	Pike back	0.5
9.	One-and-three-quarter front somersault piked	0.8
10.	Barani ball-out	0.6
	Total tariff	6.9

The next move added should be a rudi ball-out in place of the barani ball-out making the total tariff 7.1. The double full could then be added and the routine would be something similar to Routine 12.

Routine 12

1.	Half-out piked	1.0
2.	Half-out tucked	0.9
3.	Double back tucked	0.8
4.	Barani	0.5
5.	Double full	0.8
6.	Rudi	0.7
7.	Pike back	0.5
8.	Full	0.6
9.	One-and-three-quarter front somersault piked	0.8
10.	Rudi ball-out	0.8
	Total tariff	7.4

It is at this stage when it really depends upon the performer as to which moves are included in the next routine. A new move could be either a double back piked, a half-in half-out tucked or a rudi-out. It depends upon which moves the performer masters first. The next routines are therefore just

Routine Building

guide-lines as to how the tariff can be built up from 7.4 to a 10.0. It should be remembered therefore that the order in which the new moves are put into the routines will not suit every individual.

Routine 13

1.	Half-out piked	1.0
2.	Double back piked	0.9
3.	Half-out tucked	0.9
4.	Double back tucked	0.8
5.	Barani	0.5
6.	Double full	0.8
7.	Rudi	0.7
8.	Full	0.6
9.	One-and-three-quarter front somersault piked	0.8
10.	Rudi ball-out	0.8
	Total tariff	7.8

An alternative to the double back piked as the second move in Routine 13 is the half-in half-out which would make the total tariff 7.9. If the performer prefers not to work into the half-in half-out then he or she could start with it and make the first four moves of the routine:

1. Half-in half-out tucked
2. Half-out piked
3. Half-out tucked
4. Double back tucked

The next aim is to try and put both the half-in half-out and the double back piked into the same routine.

Routine 14

1.	Half-in half-out tucked	1.0
2.	Half-out piked	1.0
3.	Double back piked	0.9
4.	Half-out tucked	0.9

5.	Double back tucked	0.8
6.	Rudi	0.7
7.	Double full	0.8
8.	Full	0.6
9.	One-and-three-quarter front somersault piked	0.8
10.	Rudi ball-out	0.8
	Total tariff	8.3

Obviously a one-and-three-quarter front somersault into a rudi ball-out does not have to be used at the end of every routine but it is a good way of ending routines until performers have a wider vocabulary of double somersaults. Depending upon which way round the performer learns the moves, the half-in half-out could be replaced with a rudi-out. However, the aim should be to put both in the routine as in Routine 15.

Routine 15

1.	Rudi-out tucked	1.1
2.	Double back piked	1.0
3.	Half-out piked	0.9
4.	Half-in half-out tucked	1.0
5.	Half-out tucked	0.9
6.	Double back tucked	0.8
7.	Rudi	0.7
8.	Double full	0.8
9.	One-and-three-quarter front somersault piked	0.8
10.	Rudi ball-out	0.8
	Total tariff	8.8

Before attempting to put both rudi-outs in the routine. the rudi-out piked can replace the rudi-out tucked in routine 15 thus making the tariff 8.9. Again it may be that a performer learns the full-in half-out before the rudi-out — if this is the case then the rudi-out tucked or piked can be replaced by a full-in half-out. However, it is very rare that performers put the full-in half-out into a routine before a rudi-out. Another alternative to increase the tariff would be to include a half-in half-out piked. If performers find they are good at picking up the half-in half-out tucked they may choose to put a piked one into the routine before the full-in half-out or the rudi-out.

Routine 16 has a similar tariff to Routine 15, except it has a feet-to-feet routine rather than the one-and-three-quarter front somersault and rudi ball-out at the end.

Routine 16

1.	Rudi-out tucked	1.1
2.	Double back piked	0.9
3.	Half-out piked	1.0
4.	Half-in half-out tucked	1.0
5.	Half-out tucked	0.9
6.	Double back tucked	0.8
7.	Rudi	0.7
8.	Double full	0.8
9.	Full	0.6
10.	Full-in half-out tucked	1.1
	Total tariff	8.9

It is a good idea to include a few lower tariff moves towards the end to prepare for the finish — especially if the last move is very difficult as in Routine 16. Performers should remember that it is the last moves and the ending (whether it is controlled or uncontrolled) that sticks in a judge's mind when raising (or lowering) your score. Another handy tip performers should remember is to sandwich an easier move between two difficult moves, rather than bunching all the difficult moves together — this makes the routine easier and also helps to keep up a consistent height throughout the routine.

Routine 17

1.	Rudi-out piked	1.2
2.	Double back tucked	0.8
3.	Rudi-out tucked	1.1
4.	Half-out piked	1.0
5.	Half-in half-out tucked	1.0
6.	Half-out tucked	0.9
7.	Double back piked	0.9
8.	Rudi	0.7
9.	Double full	0.8
10.	Full-in half-out	1.1
	Total tariff	9.5

Once a performer gets to this stage in his or her career, attaining higher than a 10.0 tariff is very difficult. A performer has to work extremely hard to add a new move to the routine in order to gain an extra 0.1 or 0.2 tariff. For men, the easiest way to score above the 10.0 tariff is to include a half-out triffis (triple forward somersault with a half twist out of the third somersault) in the routine. Although the triff (as it is known) sounds daunting, it is actually much less complicated to learn than either full-in half-outs or full-in full-outs. However, it does require a great deal of height and rotation if the performer is going to successfully work out of it and so is not such a popular move with women.

To finish off, two more routines are looked at. One breaks the 10.0 tariff barrier without including the triff where as the other does include the triff.

Routine 18

1.	Half-in half-out piked	1.1
2.	Rudi-out piked	1.2
3.	Full-in full-out	1.2
4.	Half-out piked	1.0
5.	Double back piked	0.9
6.	Rudi-out tucked	1.1

Routine Building

7.	Half-in half-out tucked	1.0
8.	Half-out tucked	0.9
9.	Double back tucked	0.8
10.	Full-in half-out	1.1
	Total tariff	10.3

Routine 19

1.	Half-out triff tucked	1.3
2.	Half-in half-out piked	1.2
3.	Rudi-out piked	1.2
4.	Double back piked	0.9
5.	Rudi-out tucked	1.1
6.	Half-in half-out tucked	1.0
7.	Half-out piked	1.0
8.	Double back tucked	0.8
9.	Half-out tucked	0.9
10.	Full-in full-out	1.2
	Total tariff	10.6

Routine 20

1.	Half-out triff piked	1.4
2.	Half-in half-out triff tucked	1.4
3.	Half-out triff tucked	1.3
4.	Half-in rudi-out piked	1.3
5.	Rudi-out piked	1.2
6.	Half-in rudi-out tucked	1.2
7.	Rudi-out tucked	1.1
8.	Full-in full-out pucked	1.2
9.	Full-in rudi-out	1.3
10.	Miller straight	1.4
	Total tariff	12.8

As can be seen in Routines 18 and 19 the triff does make it much easier to attain a tariff above 10.0. To reach 12.0 and 13.0 tariffs performers need to learn half-out triffs, half-in half-out triffs and rudi-out triffs (piked and tucked). All of these moves are learned through the same progressions as the half-in half-out and rudi-out fliffis.

The ultimate for trampolining is to have it included in the Olympic games where it would earn the recognition it deserves for its skill and daring. Perhaps if trampolining is included as an Olympic sport, we will see a 14.0 tariff performed in competition.

Glossary

Like most sports, trampolining has developed its own terminology with much of its basic language usage common to diving and gymnastics. The more complicated names describing specific movements derived from America where trampolining first began as a competitive sport. This glossary gives a detailed explanation of terms used throughout the text and familiar terms used within the sport of trampolining.

Adolph   A forward somersault with three-and-a-half twists.

Amplitude   Total fulfilment of the shape.

Arch   More often referred to as a hollow position, this is when the back is hyper-extended.

Axis   An imaginary line through the centre of the body about which it rotates (during somersaults) or spins (during twists).

Back   Abbreviation for a backward somersaulting action.

Ball-out   Forward somersaulting from the back drop position.

Barani   A front somersault with a half twist — the performer does not lose sight of the bed.

Barani-in   Multiple somersault where a half twist is performed in the first somersault.

Barani-out   Multiple somersault where a half twist is performed in the last somersault.

Bed   The springy surface of a trampoline.

Blind   The time during any move where the performer loses sight of the trampoline.

Blocking   Stopping the movement of a part of the body suddenly (as used in creating rotation).

Bounce roll   A forward somersault from back to back.

Cast   Movement sideways across the trampoline — usually due to a faulty take-off.

Cat twist   A back drop followed by a full twist, returning to a back drop.

Checking   The slowing or stopping of rotation or twist.

Cody   Somersaulting action performed from a front drop landing.

Corkscrew   A back drop followed by a one-and-a-half twist with a half somersault forward to back drop.

Cowboy or Cowboying   Pulling the knees apart in the tuck position in order to gain more rotation.

Glossary

Cradle A back drop followed by a half forward somersault (giving rotation) and then a half twist to a back drop.

Crash dive A three-quarter front somersault to a back drop with the body folding at the hips at the last instant. (This movement is often followed by a ball-out.)

Dismount The safe method for leaving the trampoline.

Double bouncing Where two performers alternate their bouncing on one trampoline.

Exercise The combination of ten movements, usually referred to as a routine.

Feet to feet Any stunt or routine that is performed with a take-off from the feet and a landing on the feet.

Fliffis (plural fliffes) Any double somersault with at least one half twist.

Flying somersault Any somersaulting move where the first half of the first somersault is performed in the straight position.

Form Appearance and style of a stunt or routine.

Front Abbreviation for a forward somersaulting action.

Front one-and-three One-and-three-quarter forward somersaults from the feet to a back drop.

Full-in full-out A double somersault; with one twist in the first somersault (in) and one twist in the second (out).

Gain Movement forward away from the centre of the bed during the stunt — always in the opposite direction to any rotation.

Half-in half-out Any multiple somersaulting action where a half twist is performed in the first somersault (in) and also in the last somersault (out).

Hand spotting Assistance given by the coach or support with his or her hands.

Kaboom A somersaulting action created by one part of the body coming into contact with the bed immediately after another part.

Kick-out Extending the legs and body from a tucked or piked position, to slow down rotation in preparation for either a landing or a twist.

Killing the bounce or bed Action used to absorb the rebound of bed in order to prevent further movement.

Kipping The assisted bounce given to any performer by another person depressing the bed immediately prior to the performance of a stunt or bounce.

Layout A straight position with the body fully extended.

Lazy back A three-quarter back somersault to a front drop landing.

Line-out When a performer places straight arms along the side of the body during the kick-out, or whilst twisting in order to enhance the form.

Move   Any one skill or trick.

Miller   A triple twisting double back somersault (as first performed by Wayne Miller, USA).

Out-bounce   An extra foot bounce at the end of a routine for extra control.

Phasing   The smooth transition of defined shapes throughout a skill to show clearly take-off lift, performance of the element and recovering (or kick-out).

Pike   A body position with the legs perfectly straight, and the body folded at the hips producing a minimum angle of ninety degrees. In jumps and single somersaults the hands touch the toes and in multiple somersaults the hands are held behind the calves.

Puck   A combination of the tucked and piked shapes showing a minimum angle of ninety degrees between the body and thigh, and the thigh and lower leg. Used when performing twists in multiple somersaults.

Pullover   Backward somersaulting action from a back drop landing, initiated by closing the hip angle whilst in contact with the bed thus taking the perfomer over to the feet.

Randolph (randi)   Forward somersault straight with two-and-a-half twists.

Rig   *See* Spotting rig.

Roller   A seat drop followed by a full twist and a return to a seat drop.

Routine   Skills, stunts or tricks which are linked together through swingtime. Routines can be either compulsory or voluntary with competitions requiring ten skills.

Rudolph (rudi)   Forward somersault straight with one-and-a-half twists.

Short   Failure to perform the necessary amount of twist or rotation.

Sitting   Pushing the hips backwards during a forward take-off.

Spotting   When the take-off and the landing are performed exactly in the middle of the trampoline. Also when non-performers stand at each side of the trampoline for safety purposes.

Spotting rig   A safety harness suspended by ropes and pulleys from overhead supports (also referred to as a spotting belt). The rig can be adapted for both somersaulting and twisting.

Straddle   A position assumed in the air when the body is piked but with the legs spread wide apart.

Stuck   Difficulty in completing a move due to lack of movement or rotation. *See* Short.

Swingtime   Performing a routine, or a series of stunts, with no free bounces in between.

Swivel hips   A seat drop followed by a half twist and a return to a seat drop.

Glossary

Tag A game played by trampolinists where the first person performs a skill with each following trampolinist tagging another on. When a trampolinist fails to tag another skill on he or she is out.

Tick-tock The correct movement around the trampoline bed during a routine.

Travel Excess movement around the trampoline bed during a skill or routine.

Trick *See* Move.

Triffis (Plural triffes) Any triple somersault with at least one half twist.

Tuck A body position with the hips and knees fully flexed and the hands clasping the shins.

Turntable A front drop returning to a front drop with the body rotating horizontal in relation to the bed.

Twist Gyration of the body around its longitudinal axis (the line running from the top of the head down towards the feet).

Working the bed The correct co-ordination of the vigorous actions which are required to obtain maximum height, without loss of control.

Work-up Breaking down the whole skill into parts to aid learning (each part is called a work-up).

Wrap When a performer draws his or her arms in from an extended position to a position close to the body in order to accelerate twisting.

Useful Addresses

BTF Head Office

Rob Walker (Chairman)
152a College Road
Harrow
Middlesex HA1 1BH

Regional Offices

Scotland
Caledonia House
South Gyle
Edinburgh EH12 9DQ

North West
David Rankin (Secretary)
15 Porto Hey Road
Irby
Merseyside L61 2XA

Northern Ireland
Tim Clifford (Secretary)
65 Deramore Park South
Belfast BT9 5JY

Midlands
Irene Thompson (Secretary)
1 Brookvale Avenue
Coventry
West Midlands CV3 2DG

Wales
Kathy Stanley (Secretary)
2 Ladybench
Coed Eva
Gwent NP44 4TT

South West
Nicky Allen (Secretary)
18 Winscombe Court
Frome
Somerset BA11 2TZ

South
Fred Isaac (Secretary)
Hill Brow Main Road
Cranmore
Isle of Wight PO41 0XW

London and South East
Carol Jobson (Secretary)
33 Batchelors
Pembury
Kent TN4 2ED

East
Mark Young (Secretary)
2 Park House
Brook Road
Borehamwood
Hertfordshire WD6 5HH

Yorkshire and North Midlands
Alan Dykes (Secretary)
19 Doncaster Road
Doncaster
South Yorkshire DN3 1HP

North
Jim Crowe (Secretary)
230 Yewdale Road
Carlisle
Cumbria CA2 7SD

Index